ONCE A WARRIOR
Captain Thomas Price

Mission Alaska!

Tony Boyd Priest

ONCE A WARRIOR

Captain Thomas Price
Mission Alaska!

Copyright © Tony Boyd Priest 2013

All rights reserved in all media. No part of this book may be used or reproduced without written permission except in the case of brief quotations embodied in articles and reviews.

First Publication

Published in the United States of America

Published by

ATC Publishing LLC

P.O. Box 127

Senoia, Georgia 30276

ISBN-13: 978-0692401262

ISBN-10: 0692401261

Publishers Note: This is a work of fiction. Names, characters, places and incidents are either the products of the author's imagination or are used fictitiously. Any resemblance to actual persons, living or dead, business establishments, events, or locales is coincidental or fictionalized.

DEDICATION:

Dedicated to the Courageous Souls of our Military, Fire, Law Enforcement and Search and Rescue Men and Women, Living and Deceased and to All the Unsung Heroes of Wars Fought

And to

MY FRIENDS AND COMRADES

Table of Contents

Chapter 1   Return to Alaska
Chapter 2   Visit with an Old Comrade
Chapter 3   Nam Man
Chapter 4   There's More?
Chapter 5   Men without a Country
Chapter 6   Coming Home
Chapter 7   Alaska Arrival - The First One
Chapter 8   How This Trip Got Started
Chapter 9   In To Anchorage
Chapter 10 The Colonel
Chapter 11 The 'Team'
Chapter 12 Picking up 'Red'
Chapter 13 Back to Business
Chapter 14 Farewell, Alaska and the Bear
Chapter 15 Plans Change
Chapter 16 Lunch at Sam's Place
Chapter 17 Recon - The Search Begins
Chapter 18 Recon - Day Two
Chapter 19 Buck at Wolf Creek Mountain
Chapter 20 Discovery
Chapter 21 Trouble from Below
Chapter 22 Bob and 'Wild Bill' at Newtok
Chapter 23 Captain Jerry Bagwell
Chapter 24 The Leap Frog
Chapter 25 Surprise
Chapter 26 Mission Accomplished
Chapter 27 Last Visit with 'Buck'
Chapter 28 Warriors Return
Chapter 29 Celebration
Chapter 30 Goodbye Alaska?

Chapter 1

RETURN TO ALASKA

In the extreme quietness, deep in the snow covered Alaskan wilderness, a lone white, heavily horned Ram sheep was going about his pleasant task of delicately picking lichen from the gray granite rocks. Occasionally exposed to the warming sun, lichen provided at least some sustenance for these beautiful high altitude animals.

Suddenly alert the large Ram glanced toward a subtle yet common sound. He'd stopped chewing momentarily, watched and carefully listened for the intruder to be exposed. He tilted his head downward and over as he began to focus on the large gap in his mountain range.

As the sound increased it was apparent that it was an aircraft which would simply pass by. Once identified the Ram relaxed and continued to graze.

Suddenly, from around a large boulder a beautiful blue and white Cessna 206 appeared with a roar. Barely clearing the mountain side in a steep, right oblique turn, only the top of the airplane was visible. Then as the airplane rolled level, through the right side aircraft window, came into view the graying, mustached pilot.

A big smile broke across Captain Tom's face as he could now see 12 to 15 Dall sheep grazing among the rocks. There were several large Big Horn Rams alert and watching the aircraft's every move. All were standing precariously close to the edge of the jagged rock cliffs of the snow covered mountain.

Captain Tom Price, now in his sixties, still loved to fly, especially in the deep Alaskan wilderness and especially on this still, bright November day.

He'd once again flown across the majestic Alaska Range through the infamous Rainy Pass and was now turning westbound with the great tundra of Alaska in his view.

His plan was somewhat of a sightseeing and remembrance tour as he could have made his destination 30 minutes earlier. He just wanted to get reacquainted with some of his Alaskan flying skills and challenge himself somewhat.

As he exited the pass to follow the south fork of the Kuskokwim River, he looked below and noticed he was over Farewell Lake and that off to his left lay the mysterious town of Farewell, Alaska.

He decided to turn back, make one orbit over the town and then get back over to the river.

He remembered flying different folks, typically government types, in and out of there on occasion, but never asked them their business.

'Mysterious town he thought- Population – one... Buildings – several... Runway – 4,000 feet... Not near any village, road or river for that matter. The nearest creek is called High Power Creek, not exactly an Athabaskan name. And oh yeah, he'd never seen Farewell Lake frozen even in January. Plus, the 'unverified airstrip' a few miles northwest has a few buildings as well - for what purpose?'

"Always planned to do some looking around there someday," he mumbled to himself. "Wonder if Jed Williams is still the caretaker of Farewell, Alaska."

After completing his surveillance of Farewell, he mentally noted 'not one human being in sight', then rolled out level. With the rocky, vertical cliffs to his back he continued west.

On course again, his thoughts came back to the Kuskokwim, 'Kusko' as the locals call it. He mentally began to review all the villages and towns he'd serviced up and down the meandering, snake-like river.

'Let's see', he recalled, 'from the headwaters above Nikolai to McGrath, Stony River, Sleepmute, Red Devil, George Town, Crooked Creek, Aniak, Kalskag and Bethel... All have a story - memories both good and bad.'

He remembered the different challenges proposed by each airport under various seasonal conditions. He also reflected on the people, very hardy of course, happy, open, generous and would do anything for you kind of folks.

But since the river is over 400 miles long (all in Alaska), he knew he didn't have enough time to visit everyone.

He waggled his wings left and right to clear the area below then dove down to follow the river bed where he'd seen moose, bear, wolves and other wildlife many times.

Now at low level and going around a bend, he came upon not one but two grizzlies obviously flipping rocks along the riverbed. He banked over and buzzed by them.

"Kind of late for you guys to be out isn't it?"

He reached down and tapped his fingers on his old 12 Gauge Mossberg Pump strapped to the right seat. He smiled, looked ahead and continued west.

Deeper now in the outback of Alaska he continued his climb up to a comfortable 4,500 foot altitude. For a while, the drone of his Cessna 206 was heard only by his non-human friends.

After some time, in the distance he could see smoke rising from some of the homes in and around the village of Nikolai. As he approached, he thought about saying hello but decided rather to take a look at the town and the airstrip where he'd landed so many times.

After a one pass survey, he banked left and headed along the river westbound. "Don't have time to stop in today... Wasn't invited either," he spoke softly to himself.

He knew it was always best to let someone know if you planned to land there or at any of the outlying villages for that matter. One thing they didn't like was surprises, especially from tourists. Today he was a tourist.

After passing the town of McGrath, he continued to follow the river south looking for the confluence of the Kusko and Stony rivers.

When reaching the Stony, he continued to follow it south toward Lime Village, his final destination today.

Lime Village, he remembered, was his first duty assignment beyond the Alaska Range. 'Sparravohn and Lime - sounded more like a dessert than a destination'.

It was never anything like a dessert. Weather was typically marginal at best at either location.

Visibility was very good today and as he looked off at his two o'clock position, he could see the top of Sparravohn Mountain in the distance. The adjacent clouds blocked out the runway and the early warning radar site.

'What the heck he thought; I'll take a look, just 20 miles or so, then descend back over to Lime.'

He left the river and headed to Sparravohn Mountain. As he approached he thought about dropping in on his Air Force friends, but with no military landing permit decided to simply take a look, make a one eighty over the field and get back over to the Stony River.

Overhead, "Yep, just as I remembered, a spaceship sitting on a hillside," as he referred to the saucer shaped self-contained living and working quarters of the remote station. "You don't want to get locked out of that building in the winter," he mumbled to himself.

He took a moment to remember the pilots and crews of both civilian and military aircraft that had crashed battling the elements trying to get in or out of what's billed as one of the most dangerous airports in Alaska. He included in those thoughts some of his own experiences there under some incredible conditions. As he let those feelings seep in, he definitely felt the urge to meet that challenge and more like it once again.

As he turned back toward Lime he felt thankful to have the opportunity to be tested and still be flying in Alaska. And, most of all, he appreciated the freedom that three dimensional travel had given him most of his lifetime.

As he paralleled the river, headed back to Lime Village, he suddenly caught a glimpse of movement off to his right. As he turned slightly he could see that it was a lone musher following the riverbed toward the village.

He wasn't sure… Then said aloud, "No… Sam would be running a snow machine out to meet me, not a dog sled. Not even sure if he got my letter, and…, not much down river below Lime. That fellow's probably on a hunting trip."

He waggled his wings to the musher and continued on toward the village.

Tom was looking for his friend Sam Collins, last reported as living there; however, he'd heard the village had been completely deserted. That was at least two years ago.

As he approached his destination his alertness climbed to a higher level. 'Lime', he thought...'My spookiest landing ever!'

He recounted the memory as he approached - A much younger man then.

***

'I remember the day I was dispatched on a charter flight from Anchorage to Lime Village. I was somewhat concerned about the weather conditions. It was spring, with weather moving from the high 20's at night, to the low 40's during the peak of the day. The short runway, I felt could possibly be wet, frozen in places, or both. In other words Lime Village Airport was in break-up.

No one had been in there for a couple of weeks and my passengers were desperate to get home and to bring in much needed supplies and groceries.

I called ahead and discussed the situation with Robert, the airport manager. After some discussion it was concluded that the weather and braking action on the runway was good. Visibility was unlimited.

After a quiet, uneventful flight over the mountains, I began my let-down toward my destination. I was heavy with five people, baggage and groceries aboard. However, I knew the limitations of the Seneca II aircraft and knew I was well inside my parameters for this landing. At least I thought I knew.

As I approached, I checked in on the radio. "Lime Village Unicom, Seneca 54JW... approaching 10 miles east. Request advisory."

Robert was standing by, "Winds are calm. Pressure is 30.22.

Captain, your braking action should be good. I just drove my truck down the runway. No problem."

"Okay Robert. Thanks for your help."

As I approached for a closer look, 'I don't know if I trust that. The runway looks a little shiny which could possibly mean wet glare ice.'

I called again, "Lime Village traffic, Seneca 54JW downwind for runway Eight. Robert, did you test braking all the way down the runway? Sure looks a little wet, kinda' shiny in places."

He came back, "Yes, I did. Braking is good."

"Thanks," as I continued on to left base.

"Seneca 54JW is on left base for runway 10 Lime Village," I called.

Glancing downward momentarily, I noticed the heavy ice flow in the river. As I established my base leg, I lowered flaps to full down position and began slowing to minimum approach speed.

Now on final, I slowed to the very minimum speed and added a little power to keep from stalling, clipping the bushes at the end of the runway.

Just above stall speed now, I touched down the Seneca II exactly on the end of the 1,500 foot runway.

I held the nose off momentarily, looking for some aerodynamic braking, then gently lowered the nose and raised the manual flaps.

As I touched the brakes however.... we sped up!

I now began braking with rapid, on off brake pedal action. We were not slowing at all. 'This is not good!' I thought to myself!

I considered going around but I wasn't sure of the condition of the remainder of the runway now. I could see standing water and possibly mud ahead and felt we might not get airborne. I certainly didn't want to go plowing through mud only to end up in the river.

I could see the other end of the runway now. What I was looking at was not a pretty sight. There was no barrier at the end of the runway. From there the terrain sloped down a 30 foot embankment into a river flowing with ice.

I was still barreling toward the river and went back to full flaps... 'Got to try aerodynamics again...' With full flaps I lifted the nose off the runway. I wasn't slowing at all. 'Not good. Not good!' The end of the runway and river was coming up fast.

I kicked the rudder full to the right, hoping to get traction in a side slide and maybe some aerodynamic drag from the tail. As I slipped to the side of the runway, I kicked full left rudder and began my slide to the right. I was slowing somewhat now but it still wasn't enough. I had one more action I could do besides going into the ice jammed river.

A ground loop seemed the best option. I knew it would damage the aircraft but anything was better than going down that river bank.

I kicked full right rudder and began to spin the nose around to the right. As I passed the 90 degree point, the river was all over my windshield!

I added some power to the left engine to continue my spin around. Our momentum toward the river seemed to be subsiding as we went around.

My natural reaction to this new tail slide and to stop the spin- around was to begin powering up the right engine. It was working. It stopped the spin-around action and our momentum toward the river. I felt I was near the edge of the icy river bank, not fully stopped, but now pointed in the right direction. I continued to push both throttles forward and was at full takeoff power.

That stopped my river-bound tail slide. Now stopped, pointed in the right direction, with engines roaring, we began moving back toward the ramp area!

Within three or four seconds, now moving rapidly toward the ramp, I had to chop both throttles in order to stop and prevent us from hitting the small embankment behind the turn out area. We finally stopped in the turnaround area and were parked where we always parked. I pulled the mixtures back shutting down the engines. All was quiet.

Wow! I thought to myself. Using reverse thrust in a piston aircraft is not something one should try. But if it keeps you and your folks out of the drink, especially one with icebergs all jammed together and everything, my feeling is do it! It worked that day!

As my passengers deplaned, not a word was said until the last passenger was getting out. She was about 75 I thought.

I steadied her by holding her arm as she stepped out on the ice covered ground. She looked up, caught my eye and in broken English and with an unexcited voice," I didn't think we' za gonna make it."

"Yes Ma'am, it was a little bit slippery but... ahh, no problem!" I replied.

She held out her hand which I took gently and laid my other hand on hers with a warm gesture. She smiled, "Thanks. You can call me Mom now. Everybody else does."

I heard a heavy 'Thud!', 'Clunk!', 'Crack!' and the sound of rushing water. I knew it was the ice flow less than a hundred feet from where we stood.

As she turned and began walking away, I glanced over at the rumbling ice clogged river and let myself go there for a moment. I wondered... if you sink below the ice jammed river surface, how do you get back up through it? That is a tough one.

The last of the baggage and cargo had been unloaded and as I finished closing the doors I gave Thanks to my Maker, then thanks to my Guardian Angel - again, then charged off to find the airport operations manager. He must have been driving with chains on his tires! He was nowhere to be found.

After thoroughly checking out my muddy aircraft, especially the landing gear, I headed for home.'

***

Captain Tom chuckled, shook his head and shrugged off his thoughts as he began to descend to survey the Lime Village airport area once again.

Today was a still, bright day just as that day was.

He had been forewarned that the runway had not been maintained for some time due to so few flights in and out over the last few years. He also knew that most, if not all the folks he knew in the village during the eighties had since either died or left for the larger cities. He hadn't received any correspondence from there for quite some time.

As usual, he crossed over the short field into a downwind and carefully looked over the situation. Not a soul about it seemed.

Winds were calm. Runway looked the same, snow, with some hard to make out potholes, but with no other obstructions apparent.

He applied approach flaps, set up on the final approach leg, but eased off to the right of the runway for a low and slow pass to further scrutinize the runway.

Flying the complete length of the runway, alternately looking forward and out the left side of the aircraft, he got a good close-up view of the landing conditions.

"Terrible as usual – great for a 206," he mumbled as he added power to begin his climb out to return for a normal landing.

Back on short final now – "Before landing checks complete" as he eased the prop control forward.

He touched down smoothly on the glistening, soft snow and began his normal roll-out. Braking was good.

He turned into the small ramp area, switched off avionics and electrical, then eased the mixture back to shut off the engine.

As his prop made the last turn, he switched off the master and ignition, unbelted and opened the door.

The eerie quietness penetrated his brain.

As he glanced at the temperature gauge, "Looks about 19."

He pulled his old Wilbur's hat down over his ears and stepped out onto the frozen ground. "Still a great hat!" he said as he pulled it down more snugly. "Thanks Joe"- as he remembered Joe and Ann Wilbur, his previous employers and two wonderful folks from the old days.

He turned, reached back into the plane and released the seat belt from around his Mossberg 12 Gauge. He lifted it off the seat, turned, pointed it away and cycled a shell out onto the ground. He carefully picked it up, blew off the clinging snow and reinserted it into the tube.

He laid his shotgun across the pilot seats, then reached under the right seat and pulled out his shoulder holster with several magazines attached. After securing his holster, he reached back under the seat and pulled out his Glock pistol. Carefully, he removed the cloth wrapping, pulled a clip from his pocket and inserted it.

Stuffing the deadly weapon into his holster, he adjusted the belts for comfort.

Feeling ok with that, he put on his heavy bomber jacket, zipped up, then put his hands together and blew into them momentarily and quickly pulled on his heavy gloves.

As he completed his post flight walk-around inspection, he glanced over at the mostly frozen river, the ice was now primarily flat and smooth, typical for this time of year.

Feeling his aircraft was secure, he glanced up the hill toward where the people, his friends, had usually come down to meet his mail plane. Today, no one came down. He saw their faces momentarily laughing, talking and smiling with anticipation.

He shook his head. Contemplating, he again picked up his Mossberg shotgun, left the parking pad and headed up the small hill on the old roadway. As he entered the village he didn't see a soul.

"Hello!"... He yelled.

There was no response.

He walked on down the old dirt now snow covered street, looking at the abandoned, falling down homes. Finally, he stopped and gazed at a home off to his right he thought looked familiar.

As he knocked on the door, it moved slightly open.

"Hello, anyone here? he asked. He pushed the door fully open and discovered that indeed this was the house where 'Mom' had lived most of her years.

As he entered, he noticed the table where he'd had a meal or two. Off to his left was the old wood stove where she usually had a pot of coffee brewing. As he stepped forward on the squeaky floor, he glanced over into the back room. There he saw the old washing machine she was so proud of.

He let himself go there for a moment and remembered what a nurturing and caring lady she was. As he glanced back into the kitchen, he could almost smell the fresh coffee brewing.

"Looks like all the old folks have passed on," Tom said quietly. What a shame he thought. 'Kids all went off to college or moved to Anchorage, Fairbanks, or to the Lower 48. As the families split up, the older generations simply lost hope. It wasn't just here but throughout Alaska that entire villages had completely disappeared.'

"What's the answer?" he contemplated.

Shaking his head, he pulled his collar up around his neck and turned to walk out.

Before he closed the door, he turned one last time as if to say goodbye. He visualized Mom's smile as she stood by the old wood stove. He raised his arm as if to wave, then turned and gently pulled the door shut without looking back.

CHAPTER 2

VISIT WITH AN OLD COMRADE

As he stepped outside, he heard slipping and sliding of dogsled runners on the ice, echoing from the river below. As he listened closer he heard the panting of dogs obviously in full run across the icy terrain.

"Wow, that guy's making good time," he spoke softly to himself.

He hurriedly headed across the road and looked down the hillside toward the river.

"That looks like Sam's parka," he mumbled.

He was about to yell when he saw the sled team swing left toward the air strip.

"Must be Sam! He got my letter," He said aloud.

Anticipating meeting an old friend, he began the half mile walk back down the hill toward his airplane.

As he approached, the team had already arrived and was sitting quietly as the owner was tending to them.

"Sam?"   "Is that you?" Tom yelled as he paused momentarily resting his shotgun on his left arm.

As the musher turned and pulled back his fur lined parka, "No Sir, I'm Will."

There he was, a spitting image of Sam just 30 years younger.

"I'm sorry; you must be Sam's youngest son," said Tom.

"That's right. You Captain Tom?" He asked.

"That's right," replied Tom.

"Where's your Dad?   He's still around isn't he?" questioned Tom.

"Yes Sir, sure is. We've got a place just up the river," said Will.

Will made a clicking noise and picked up his dog's attention, then glancing back over at Tom, "Say, aren't you the 'Iceman'? Didn't you used to fly in here a lot?"

"Well, some guys down in Anchorage gave me that handle. It wasn't because I had nerves of steel as the name indicates. It was because I was so broke; I'd show up in any kind of weather."

"Oh," replied Will.

"Well, maybe a little valor there in that I really cared about the folks out here and always did my best to get the supplies in. Course, I did have a rep for dragging the most ice ever seen on an airplane into Valdez one time," said Tom.

"Yeah... You also have a rep for the scariest landing ever performed or witnessed by anyone in our village," remarked Will.

"Yeah, I know that. I was thinking about that a little while ago as a matter of fact," he chuckled, "I thought of it every time I was about to land here after that day," said Tom.

"Well, Dad's mentioned you from time to time - said you had a lot of things in common," said Will.

"Sure do," answered Tom.

"Say, any chance we could get on up to your place and visit for a spell," questioned Tom, "I don't mind walking."

"We'd planned on your coming out and staying a couple of days. The dogs can easily pull both of us. It's just a few miles upriver," said Will.

"Sounds good," answered Tom.

As Tom glanced at his aircraft, "I've got covers and I noticed there's a red devil heater over in the shed."

"OK – yeah. The red devil does work. Once in a while we get someone in here. They generally stay overnight up at 'Mom's place. I guess she had a lot of pilot kids back in the old days," said Will.

"Yeah… I was one of them," answered Tom.

"I sure hate seeing the village deserted," Tom said as he shook his head.

"Yeah, me too," Will remarked.

Tom with Will's assistance proceeded to secure the aircraft and apply the covers onto the wings, tail and windshield.

Tom opened the door, reached inside for one last check. He eased the mixture levers forward and the throttles to the perfect starting position.

Will closely watched the process with interest.

"Cables and controls freeze on occasion… Need to be in the go position," Tom explained.

After a last glance around the aircraft, they headed toward the waiting dog sled.

"Just take a seat Captain," Will instructed as he gestured to the sled. "Sun's going down within the hour but not to worry though, there's still enough light these days to see the trail. The dogs know the way home anyway," said Will.

"OK," Tom smiled and nodded his head as he ambled toward the sled. Tom climbed in and settled down into the bottom of the comfortable sled seat.

As he pulled the heavy bear hide blanket up to his chin he was somewhat startled as Will yelled to his dogs... "MUSH!"

They jolted ahead leaving the airstrip and deserted village quickly behind.

As they cruised along the riverside trail, Tom felt he was finally back in the true Alaskan wilderness.

***

After a time and having put a few miles behind them, Tom and Will had talked a lot and had become more relaxed with each other. They both now felt they'd known each other for years.

As the conversation eventually dwindled, Tom dozed off and let some of his Alaskan memories flood into his consciousness.

'Sparravohn and Lime - Flight 302, one they flew daily from Anchorage to the area - was always an adventure of some sort. One particular flight stood out in his mind as he remembered the time he surveyed the group of folks getting ready to board his twin Cessna 402 aircraft in Anchorage.

Let's see - four Native Americans, one with baby, one with a large box of live baby chicks, one well-dressed Husky with a red scarf around his neck, an Air Force Captain and ... a Bird Colonel, both carrying briefcases.

Now that was quite a mixture even for Alaska. He remembered the look on the officers faces as boarding began.

The boarding agent sounded perplexed as well... "Flight 302 now boarding... anyone with small children ... followed by folks with chickens... or Air Force Officers ... Oh, what the heck, the plane is leaving. Everybody get on."

I thought, "Terri!" as I glanced over at the blue eyed, rather attractive brunette at the podium. She must have felt my thought, as she looked up and gave me that humorous smile. What an awesome agent and friend she was.

After getting everyone settled and after a short briefing, we taxied out into the night slowly becoming day.

As we cleared the Anchorage Bowl area, most of the passengers had become enamored by the spectacular scenery. Both below and on both sides of the aircraft, the morning sun infiltrated the mountain peaks of the Alaska Range and splashed its brilliance onto the white snow.

On the route that day, after clearing the Alaska Range and entering the Tundra area, he remembered there were Caribou by the thousands.

The migrating herds were grazing along, brown and beautiful against the blue ponds and lakes, the green meadows and the streaks of white snow which seemed to finish the beautiful portrait. It was an unforgettable, almost spiritual picture and was forever etched in his memory.'

***

A lurch in the sleds movement suddenly jolted him out of his light sleep.

He sat up exposing his face to the icy cold night air.

Will had slowed the team as he approached a stream where the river's water was flowing over the ice, "Captain Tom, You up for a stop? I'd like to give the dogs a breather - check this ice up ahead."

"I'm great Will. You're a good driver. The ride's very comfortable," answered Tom.

They stopped. Will set the brake and walked ahead into the night. Tom pushed back his bear skin cover and climbed out onto the crisp snow. He stretched his arms upward then outward to get better circulation going. Then he placed his leg forward onto the side of the sled, a martial arts exercise he'd done a thousand times before.

He stood there stretching, listening into the quietness.

The sound of Will's boots crunching on the frozen trail became louder as he came walking back, "Looks fine ahead Captain."

The dogs panting had subsided and the stillness of the night began to set in. As they stood there for a moment, both were mesmerized by the fragrant smell of evergreens and the crisp clean feeling of the icy air. Silence began to settle into their deepest cores.

Will pulled back his parka and looked upward at the stars.

Overhead, there were at least a million stars stretching from horizon to horizon with no city lights to distract from their brightness.

"Look at that Captain," said Will as he carefully scanned the brilliance. "Heard there was no end to what we're seeing out there. Doesn't seem quite right does it... Can't really understand it - Makes me feel like a speck of dust down here."

They both gazed at the spectacular sight.

"Captain, I would think you would have some insight on the universe out there with your 30,000 hours of flying airplanes. What's that, three or four solid years in the sky?" questioned Will.

"Yeah, something like that," replied Tom.

"You know Will," he continued. "In my estimation, it goes way beyond our just being able to be up there."

"You know, I've been out many nights, checked out the stars many, many times and for a time in my life, avoided looking at them simply because I just felt small, so small that I understood each of us was, as you mentioned, a speck of dust against the whole picture."

Tom continued, "Then, one night, sitting alone by a dying camp fire, I cautiously leaned back to gaze at the stars.

Right at that moment, I heard a message, perhaps a Divine message for me to share with others.

Would you like to hear it?" asked Tom.

"Sure would," answered Will.

"It went something like this..."

'Yes, Tom. You're right. Every man is a speck of dust in relation to the Universe. However, you – your life, is your speck of dust. What you do with it is determined by you. Be the best you can be in all aspects of your life. Manage it well, physically, mentally, spiritually and financially.'

"I was quite surprised at that of course but I was relieved to get an understanding from that perspective," stated Tom.

"Well, now that you put it that way, I believe you're right about that," answered Will.

"Guess we'd better get underway if you're ready," suggested Tom.

As Tom climbed back aboard, Will clicked and the dogs quickly aligned themselves with ears raised.

As Will got the dogs back in motion, "Thanks Captain Tom. I'll consider your words. It's still a little scary to think about though."

"Well, not as scary as sliding across this ice with water flowing over the runners," said Tom as he peered over the side of the sled.

Will grinned, "Mush... Mush..."

Tom looked up at the brilliant heavens again, saw a shooting star, smiled, then pulled the parka down over his face and slid back down into the warm comfort of his bear skin cover.

The gentle rocking let him relax and doze off again.

***

He was again awakened as the dogs became excited and picked up the pace.

As they proceeded down the final hill into more open terrain, he could see well ahead that up on the other side of the shallow valley there was a large log home.

All the windows were lighted which made him feel welcome. He noticed a nice column of smoke coming from the chimney.

Several barns sat back away from the river but were still close to the house. A little further up the river he could see two smaller houses with smoking chimneys as well.

Two bon fires up river and down river illuminated the entire property quite well.

As they approached, he could see a large corral behind the main barn and noticed the silhouettes of several horses.

As they got closer to the house, he glanced over his shoulder and saw a couple of dog pens set between the barns. There appeared to be young pups in this one, older dogs in the second.

The dogs continued to bark as the sled slipped by them. The dogs pulling the sled ignored the others as if they were on a serious mission. Actually, Tom surmised that they were probably quite exhausted after an arduous journey.

As they pulled up and stopped in front of the house, the large main cabin door swung opened.

Sam stepped out onto the porch.

"What cha got Will?" He asked.

"An old friend Dad," answered Will.

Captain Tom slowly pulled the parka away from his head.

"Captain Tom!" Sam exclaimed..."You old dog! What are you doing in these parts?"

"Just out reminiscing - seeing what's left of our world," replied Tom as he quickly climbed out of the sled.

"Well, as you noticed, our home in the suburbs has become the center of town," exclaimed Sam as he walked quickly to meet Tom.

There was a quick handshake and military like hug with a slap on the back.

"Come on in Tom!" Sam said.

"Thanks Sam. You look good," replied Tom.

"Shut up!" Sam said with a huge grin.

As Captain Tom stepped onto the porch, through the open door, he could see a large room sporting a large, glowing stone fireplace.

Pausing on the porch, Tom turned to Will who was working diligently with the dogs, "Will that was quite a nice ride. Thanks."

Will looked up, "totally my pleasure. I enjoyed it as well. Good to finally meet you."

As they turned to walk in, "Sam, that's quite a nice boy you've got there. Kind of reminds me of you a few years back."

"Thanks Tom. Mae and I both would agree with you," answered Sam.

As Tom entered, looking around the large room, he waved his arm in a summary gesture, "Your house expounds warmth and good feeling."

Sam smiled and nodded. "Thanks. We owe it to the lady of the house of course. If it wasn't for her, this would probably look like a barracks or hunter's cabin at best."

As they were about to close the door, Will, in a hurried manner, made his way in out of the cold.

After all had entered, Sam turned and dropped the large safety beam down across the door. "Bear lock," as he glanced up at Tom.

The 'Lady of the House', Mae, entered into the room, greeted her son and husband first, then acknowledged their guest. "You must be the famous Captain Tom."

Tom stepped forward to meet her.

As he reached out, "Mae, I am glad to meet you!"

'She's attractive for her age, half Caucasian, half Athabaskan he supposed. He remembered her from another village, possibly further north, from some years ago. He was amazed that Sam had landed such a beautiful lady for his wife'.

She smiled and put out her hand. Tom took her hand and placed his left hand over the top of hers in a continuing warm gesture.

As he released her hand, "Sam, you are a lucky man."

"Yes I am," Sam agreed enthusiastically.

"How about some coffee?" Sam asked.

"Sounds wonderful. Decaf I suppose - given the hour," replied Tom.

"Mae, how about whipping up some coffee for my old friend?" asked Sam.

Mae smiled," I'd be happy to," as she turned toward the kitchen.

Then she glanced back at the guest, "Of course you are staying over tonight. We have a nice bedroom upstairs," as she gestured toward a large rustic ladder leaning against the loft entrance.

Sam broke in," Sorry Tom. My sons and I built this whole place, never got into staircases though."

"Awe, that works just fine Sam," Tom commented as he glanced up the ladder.

"Yeah, I reckon I could stay over tonight," he continued. Didn't plan on coming in this late - but since you asked... I'd be happy to... Ladder's fine."

As Mae reentered the living room, "I've got the coffee brewing and actually we were about to have dinner Tom. Are you hungry?"

"I could eat a horse," exclaimed Tom!

Mae and Will questioningly glanced at Sam.

"It's just a figure of speech, chuckled Sam. He doesn't want to eat your horse." They all laughed.

Mae signaled to Will and called, "Let's move the table over closer to the fire."

They all moved their chairs back, then each took a corner of the large homemade table and sat it next to the fireplace.

The guys pulled the chairs back in place and sat down. Mae hurriedly went back into the kitchen.

After a few minutes, she returned with several dishes of steaming hot food.

They all ate and enjoyed each other's company.

"Mae, haven't had a dinner like that since...forever.... That Grouse hen, as well as the vegetables, was quite tasty," remarked Tom.

"Thank you Tom. I'll get some more coffee," said Mae.

"Thank you." said Tom.

Will broke in, "Dad, when did you meet Captain Tom?"

Somewhat surprised, Sam answered, "Well, actually goes all the way back to the late '60's."

Sam began to focus on the direction of the conversation as he contemplated and rubbed his chin.

Looking over at Tom, "Will's been asking me to tell him some stories about the old days in the military and especially Vietnam."

"Out here, they're taught some wartime histories, including the wars in the Gulf, just not a lot about our era," he concluded.

"Yeah, a lot of that war has only been documented in the last few years, plus, the film crews were few and far between in those days," remarked Tom.

"Well, ever since the school closed at the village, we've had to mostly home school Will. His two brothers, Tom and Abe managed to graduate with High School Diplomas from our two room school house. Can you imagine?"

"We had to send Will down to Anchorage for a few special classes and he graduated two years ago."

"Anyway, he's been talking about hearing some firsthand stories about some of our adventures for weeks, ever since he heard you were coming, "continued Sam.

"Mae, are you ok with hearing some of our stories as well?" asked Tom.

"Yes, I would like to know more. Sam's only spoken a few times about those years," answered Mae.

"Well, as your dad mentioned," said Tom looking back at Will, "we do go way back to 1967."

"In hostile country, you get to be family with the guys that save your bacon several times," Tom continued.

Sam rubbed his chin again, "You know, not too many people know the whole story behind this man either," as he gestured toward Tom.

He continued, "I'm happy to have shared some adventures and to be part of a few chapters in his life as well."

"Sure you want to go there Sam?" Tom asked.

"Not really," replied Sam. "But Will wants to know something about that time and there are a couple of stories that probably should be told and remembered by this generation."

"Mind if I record the conversation?" asked Will as he stood up.

"No, I don't care," Tom replied nodding to Sam.

Will charged off to get his recorder.

As he returned to the table he quickly pressed the record button and glanced up at his two uncomfortable subjects.

"You go ahead Tom. You're the best story teller," said Sam.

"Not so sure about that, but I can start off," answered Tom as he began, "Will, your Dad and I both have a few battle scars. It's a miracle we're here at all. He pointed and drug his right forefinger from his right cheekbone downward and under his chin following a faint scar. Between the two of us, we've both been shot, stabbed, sliced, bitten, blown up, bayoneted, blown into a bunker, blown out of a bunker, not to mention the bad food we got in Cambodia, I mean Thailand."

They both shook their heads and shrugged.

"You still carrying that shrapnel in your leg?" asked Sam.

"Yeah, don't speak of it much. Think I'll hold on to it till the price of shrapnel goes up. Then I'll cash it in. It's part of my retirement program," Tom said humorously.

"Anyway, here goes."

Chapter 3

NAM MAN

Captain Tom began to recall,

"Well, Will, you know in the late 70's and early 80's, most of our friends in Alaska were Vietnam combat veterans. It was good to be here in that these folks appreciated us for the kind of men we were. Plus, it felt great to be working alongside our brothers again."

"Just to give you a little political background Will, our Country during the Cold War era was fighting the Communist threat in any way and anywhere possible, basically defending our own way of life."

"We were able to hold a line for South Korea at the end of the Korean War and could have eventually done the same for South Vietnam which was also a self-proclaimed Independent Republic."

"As most veterans agree, we were winning our war. After Tet in 1968 there was very little of the Viet Cong army left. And, although we continued to win our battles, politically, our Country, facing all the internal pressures, eventually decided to quit. Even one of the North Vietnamese Generals later on said he was puzzled as to why we had pulled out. We had for all practical purposes totally defeated them."

One of the main reasons we were over there, just like in today's world, we've always tried to take the fight to our enemies before they come knocking on our doors."

"On a personal level, Will, when our generation went off to war in the 60's, most of us were just out of high school. It was the height of the war and the draft was in place, however, your Dad and I both volunteered right after graduation."

"And for us kids that lived in the country, we stepped off the school bus for the last time and 30 days later we were in boot camps. With no chance to build roots at home, our comrades soon became our families."

"When we lost one of them, a little more of us died inside. And, no we were not the same when we came home...caused a lot of grief for us but especially for our families. You may know the statistics. Our country lost 58,272 soldiers in combat. Afterwards tack on another 50,000 deaths in the first few years after the war ended from Agent Orange complications, drug over-doses and suicides. Regretfully, we're at the stage of losing around 400 Vietnam Veterans every day. Out of almost 3,000,000 that served, there's only 800,000 or so still alive."

"I'm not much on numbers Tom, but, I think that if two-thirds are already gone," interrupted Sam, "then almost 2,000,000 have passed on and you and I must be in the remaining one-third... Kinda puts new meaning to 'Thank a Vet'."

"Yeah, we're in the remaining one-third, but by the Grace of God, vitamin and mineral supplements and working out three times a week, maybe we can hang in there and be included in the last couple hundred or so," answered Tom.

Sam shrugged his shoulders and shook his head, "Well I'm certainly with you on that one."

Tom continued, "Anyway, that's certainly enough background in general about our cause and where we were coming from in those days."

"About your Dad and I..." continued Tom as he glanced over at Sam,

"Well... Where your dad and I come in was a time we'd both been in country for about eight months. We weren't in the same unit at the time and both had previously seen quite a bit of action."

"Now that I think about it, we actually first met at night around 200 feet in the air at the edge of a rice patty - somewhat of an extreme circumstance. I'll tell you, that night turned out to be my worst ever. It was also the last combat action I would see in South Vietnam...Nothing like saving the worst for last."

"You ready for this one?" Tom glanced at Sam.

"Yeah, go ahead," Sam said with a sigh.

***

"It was during the Tet offensive of 1968. One of our helicopters had been shot down about 13 miles northwest of Hue. It's pronounced 'Way' but spelled HUE and is the old Imperial Capital City of Vietnam. Located about 20 miles south of the old DMZ, it's in about the middle of Vietnam today. My team was sent out for a 'Recon', which is short for a reconnaissance mission, to check for any sign of the crew and attempt to recover some documents hidden in it.

The crash had occurred a few days before and no one had been able to rescue the crew due to heavy fighting on several fronts. We'd lost nine helicopters at Hue the first day of the offensive and we'd been partially overrun at Gia Le several times but managed to keep it together.

We'd volunteered for the mission especially in the hope of finding some sign of the crew.

Just a couple of days before, Operations reported an estimated 50,000 North Vietnamese regulars had infiltrated into the Northern I Corp area. Although it was hard to believe those numbers, I surmised from the heavy firepower hitting our compound that it was probably correct and I estimated that we might have some difficulty getting home on this one.

The pilot of our only remaining helicopter, although wounded, had managed to land his crippled aircraft back inside our compound. The copilot and new captain volunteered to run us out and drop us a couple of miles short of the crash site.

As the battle at Hue continued to rage, at nightfall, with some basic repairs completed, we departed and skirted around the city avoiding any of the ugly fireworks we could see.

Shortly, we found ourselves slipping down the ropes into a thick canopy of trees.

All that went well and from there we decided to simply blend into the jungle and lay low for the night.

That turned out ok as well, with no Tigers or Green Bamboo Vipers coming after us; plus, there were no Charlie or Regulars.

The next morning, after several hours of slow silent movement, we finally made it to the site.

The helicopter was mostly destroyed and was sitting on top of a lot of thick vines somewhat tilted on its side. The entire scene was eerily quiet.

It was amazing to us that the enemy had left the crashed helicopter virtually unguarded. They probably had more important things to do.

As we were very suspicious of the situation, we split up to set up a perimeter and from the thick underbrush, watched for any sign of Charlie for some time.

After no activity was observed, we cautiously moved in, carefully checking for trip wires and other booby traps.

We discovered only one trip wire near the cockpit, disarmed it, climbed in and recovered the documents hidden under the plating.

I signaled the guys in to regroup and discuss any findings.

One of them reported he had found tracks heading north, whereas, we worked in that direction for several hours. We'd hoped to catch up to them and rescue the pilots and crew; however, later on we came upon vehicle tracks.

We knew we'd been following a trail that was a couple of days old and now discovered they were traveling in a vehicle. Our idea of rescuing the crew was greatly diminished. One of the guys mumbled, "They're halfway to Hanoi by now."

With no way to get the crew and no way of knowing how far away they were, we headed back toward our designated pick up point.

We'd made it back to the helicopter crash site and were continuing south when we received a dreaded radio call.

***

"Bad news guys... LZ's too hot and they're screaming for us back in Town."

"Roger that!" Bill, our radioman answered.

As he shook his head, "Captain, we're on our own."

***

We huddled together to discuss a strategy and after checking our map and latest intelligence, we changed course and headed directly to Gia Le.

My right hand man, Peter Williams, 'Pete', was a comrade and friend I'd met in training down at Pendleton in California. He was from Southern California and introduced me to some surfing moves in between our training stints.

We'd shared the same hooch for several months at Gia Le. He was an excellent chess player by the way. Never could beat him.

Bill Rollins, my radio man, was from New York City and was counting the days till he could head home. We'd all three come over on the same flight from California, took the same convoy from DaNang to Phu Bai and made our way on our own over to the base.

We'd been on several missions, been in several firefights and all three of us were now within a couple of months of our rotation back home.

The other four were Al Torlando, Jeff Karlane, Robert Faith and Charles Hunter. All were new to the unit.

We'd worked our way through some unbelievable gnarly jungle terrain, made pretty good time at first and then ended up traveling only at night mostly due to Charlie and NVA activity. At that point, we'd been stuck out in the bush over three days. We were getting pretty fatigued and our C-rations were mostly depleted.

The last night, it was as dark a night as you could imagine.

We'd managed to get within five or six miles of Gia Le, hiding out here and there as we watched North Vietnamese regulars marching straight down Highway One, the road toward Hue.

When we were finally able to slip across the road, we dropped into an irrigation ditch which we followed and ended up in a 10 by 20 foot natural shallow foxhole adjacent to a very large rice patty.

We knew the VC were hunting us by now and estimated they could be getting pretty close.

What we didn't count on was a strategic move by a savvy enemy.

Bill had touched my elbow and pointed out the first lantern. We hit the ground observing now two, then five, then more showing up all along both tree lines.

They had silently flanked us blocking our retreat on three sides, leaving us up against a very open killing field.

Although we had our maps and intelligence reports, they obviously knew the lay of the land better than any of us.

***

Lying flat on my stomach, I could smell the jungle... the mud... the nearby rice patty. 'Must be about midnight.' I thought as I wiped some splattered mud from my watch face... '13 past midnight.'

Thought I heard a sound... My buddy Pete was next to me but I couldn't see him or hear a breath. Suddenly, the 'thunk' sound of a mortar being fired, then, a brilliant flare overhead - night became day – a whistle – mud sloshing on three sides as a Company of VC charged in for the kill.

They closed in quickly, but we were able to use the depth of the wide ditch for some protection. As we stood side by side their own illumination worked more to our advantage than theirs. Line after line fell from our deadly M-16's.

Pete yelled, "They're still coming!

"Behind us!" he screamed, as he spun around where two of our guys had fallen.

More VC were coming now from all three directions, jumping over their fallen comrades.

"Getting low on Ammo!!" I heard through the noise.

Rounds were crisscrossing around us, between us and through us. Didn't know who had been hit. Firing stopped off to my left side. I think at that point all of us had been hit at least once. It was suddenly quiet.

We fixed bayonets and waited for the VC to make a final charge on our position.

Pete and I agreed to stay back to back and try to last as long as possible. Becoming a prisoner was not an option. None wanted to go through the torture that would come as a P.O.W.

Then a whistle signaling their comrades to close in for the kill... Taking prisoners was not on their minds. They were in a mad frenzy! Bullets were zipping in every direction.

A round slammed me in the back. I lurched forward from the impact, then,

"Grenade!!!" Pete screamed, as the splash of a live grenade hit the mud behind me and to the right a couple of feet from my right leg. I turned to reach for it but my feet were stuck solidly in the muck.

Suddenly Pete dove for it – stuffed it under his belly in the mud. "Whoosh," as he rose up out of the mud two feet, then settled.

I was the last one still firing as the Cong closed in for the final kill.

Thinking of home now – one clip left. I let it go taking down a few others. As the last round left my M16, I reached for my 45! Took out the closest two or three. One round left… I quit firing and dropped to my knees in the mud just below the rim of our 'foxhole.'

The scene from above must seem horrific I thought – six dead GI's with one left in the center of what must appear from above to be a portrait of a crop circle.

The enemy fire stopped suddenly. All was quiet. My first thought was they assumed we were all dead, however found out momentarily that wasn't the case.

A minute or so passed.

Then, a voice piercing the night –

A strong, southern drawl voice came crackling over our half submerged radio. "Hey… Comrades! This is 'Spooky', and for you fellows listening, beating up on our guys, Puff - The… Magic Dragon! - Or, in other words, your worst nightmare!"

"Keep your heads down boys – This won't take a minute… And, thank you Charlie for lighting up the night."

'Bill must have gotten off a radio call in the blind just before he caught the last round.'

I hit the deck!

"BUUUUUURRRRRR!" … like the Dragon was cold, a sound like no other. I knew this battle was over when the steel rain began to fall.

The VC that could began running for any cover they could find. There wasn't much.

As he proceeded around with the 6,000 rounds per minute Gatling, the circle of death broadened, however red tracers as well continued to fly upward toward the dark silhouette of the aircraft.

Even though they were being fired upon, the Dragon crew continued to move the laser like beam lazily side to side until all ground fire ceased.

How many died... I don't know.

Suddenly quiet now – only the drone of the C47 engines could be heard.

Then, "Dust Off will be over here shortly boys... Gotta go."

I pried the mike from the radioman's frozen grip, "Thanks Spooky. Looks like only one of us left."

"Sorry Capt'n." he replied in a somber voice.

The sound of silence stabbed into the darkening night.

I worked my boots free of the mud and worked my way over to Pete.

I saw a movement.

Scrambling for my flashlight, I kneeled down and rolled him partially over. He groaned, then raised a bloody arm.

I wiped the mud from his face and eyes. He looked up at me.

"Pete! You okay?" I asked. "How'd you do that?"

"Awe, stuck that grenade down in the mud as far as I could reach. Just barely got my hand out," groaned Pete.

"You crazy fool! You could've been killed," Tom said.

"No, you're the crazy one for standing up in the line of fire," answered Pete.

He pointed down at my shirt and pants, "Look at you!"

I shined the light. Blood covered my riddled uniform. "Dang – Didn't know I had that many holes in me."

***

Both their eyes began to close as they simultaneously collapsed face down in the mud - then darkness and silence.

***

The thumping of the air caused Tom to slowly open his eyes. He rolled over and listened to the unmistakable sound of a Huey Dust-Off helicopter becoming more and more prominent.

***

I rolled over to see the dimly lit Huey homing in on what was left of our Team. I threw the smoke grenade toward the most open spot I could see to mark the best landing zone.

As the helicopter descended down to us, I could hear a few shots pinging on the blades. Evidently there was some VC that remained, hoping to do some damage through their long range shots.

As soon as the skids hit the ground, the medics came charging toward us.

Don't remember a lot about things from there, with the exception of, as we both were carried by the front of the helicopter, I observed the name below the pilot's window.... 'Captain Timothy Kohl'.

I thought what a small world this is. It was Captain Tim, a close friend from high school, Class of '64. I'd heard he had made it into the Warrant Officer Program and had become a Med-Evac Pilot.

I thought back for a moment..... 'He was always the studious one, hardworking, taking care of business kinda guy. Never a harsh or negative word came from him at any time. He'd grown up on a large Dairy Farm near our home town and I always thought that he must have had a wonderful family to become such a great person at such a young age. I felt quite proud of him at that moment.'

Both Pete and I were in and out of consciousness. The medics loaded us on board as the rest of the team members were placed in the back.

I thought 'At least all our Team's aboard.'

As Tim lifted the heavy helicopter off and began his climb out, lying on my side, I could see an acre of bodies in the shadows of the dying flares.

One of the Medics yelled, "Dang Man! You guys must have wiped out half the Cong army! They're everywhere!"

"Wasn't all us... The Dragon was here... Must've been from Georgia as well... Had that southern drawl voice," I groggily commented.

Pete tilted his head toward me. "Can we go home now?

"Yeah Pete. Let's go home."

***

"Suddenly, things got pretty exciting again as a couple of rockets went by barely missing our rotor blades.

As Tim rolled his helicopter on its side to avoid one of them, I soon realized there were two helicopters involved when a Huey Gunship zoomed in just below us and got between us and the enemy firing on us.

Your dad was the pilot on that Gunship and really let them have it with his Gatling gun and several rockets.

Finally, Tim was able to gain some altitude and with your dad flying cover, managed to break contact."

Looking over at Sam, "It's unbelievable what you and Tim and others went through to pull guys out of some really bad situations. If I remember correctly you did some pretty fancy flying that night - took some hits yourself but routed out the last of them."

"You bet. We let go with just about everything we had before we broke off... Gave them some payback for you and your guys and the downed helicopter crew as well," answered Sam.

***

"Well, finally things seemed to get quiet and I must have dozed off. Later on I awoke to a gentle pressing on my chest. I opened my eyes and I remember Captain Tim leaning over me,

"Tom, we're on the ground in DaNang and you'll be in the hospital shortly. Looks like you've got a ticket home, and... You'll probably get to do some fishing before I get back but don't catch them all... Save a few for me. Okay?" continued Tim.

"Will do. Say, when's your tour up? We definitely need to get together when you get home," I asked.

"Sure do, but, may be more than a year before I get home," Tim continued. "I'm getting transferred down to Long Binh next week," as he gestured south... "Guess they're pretty shorthanded."

As they continued to walk toward the triage tent, Tom's gaze began to settle on other helicopters bringing in wounded and dead.

Tim observed him looking at the other helicopters, some being washed out by throwing buckets of water inside to clean out the blood. He said quietly, "We're a long way from the Future Farmers of America aspect of our lives aren't we?" commented Tim.

"We definitely are," answered Tom somberly, "Never thought we'd be caught in a nightmare like this."

Then, he turned to face his rescuer and friend, "Tim... I'll be looking to hear from you." They reached and shook hands.

"You bet," answered Tim.

"Thanks for getting us out of there," concluded Tom

Tim smiled, "See you back in Georgia."

***

"As we were at the entrance to the tent, I noticed your dad holding a couple of IV bags over my head, "Pretty tough go out there Captain. We'll get you home soon."

"Yeah, Thanks."

Tim spoke up from somewhere behind, "That's Sam, the pilot of the Huey Gunship that got between us and the Cong... Not sure if we would have made it otherwise."

"Thanks to you as well Captain Sam. From what I could see, that was a pretty risky maneuver, but successful and quite the fireworks," Tom concluded

"Glad I could be there," said Sam.

I glanced to the left as several medics rushed by with Pete's stretcher.

I was finally warm and dozed off.

***

"It seemed a day or so later that your dad checked in at the Hospital in DaNang to see how things were going, talk a little. I was still highly medicated, a couple of bullet wounds and a substantial amount of shrapnel in my left leg. He'd given me the news about Pete and that his remains had already been sent home."

"Besides the Chaplin, your dad was my only visitor for several weeks. He surely helped me work through some tough realizations."

"We've been friends ever since," concluded Tom.

"If that doesn't beat all dad!" exclaimed Will. "Never heard that story... Never realized what you had been through really...Seems quite a miracle that any of you lived through that. It must have been tough to lose those friends too," concluded Will.

Both Sam and Tom nodded in contemplation.

Will continued, "You know, I've seen a lot of dad's pictures from Vietnam, but it's just hard to comprehend what level of intensity you must have experienced there... Especially, to graduate from high school with all your friends, spend a couple of weeks with your family, then end up on a plane headed for war."

"No need to try Will," said Sam as he slid his chair back from the table, "It's pretty much impossible for someone who's not been there, but, we," as he gestured toward Tom, "have respect for both you and your mom for your interest in and respect you have for us and all those who served there."

Mae, after a moment of her own thoughts and wanting to change the subject, "You've been friends a long time Sam. What did you do after Vietnam?"

Sam answered, "Well, if you and Will would like to hear a couple more stories..."

Tom followed, "Yeah, there are a couple of highlights of our post-Vietnam history probably worth mentioning."

"Here goes," Tom continued. "Right after my tour ended abruptly, I was shipped back to the states and watched the rest of the war on TV.

And, your dad ..," as he looked to Sam for input.

Sam continued, "Yeah, I got two weeks leave and accompanied Tom home at the end of February '68, then went back, stayed for about six more months and planned to stay longer. I'd had plenty of good saves and had been pretty lucky so far," Sam continued, "But when Tim went in for the second and final time over in Quang Tin, I figured it was about the right time for me to hang it up. I'd gotten to be close friends with him and his Crew Chief Hernandez also killed that day."

"You know Tim completed somewhere around 800 missions and managed to pull out more than 1,600 wounded from the field."

He was quite a pilot as well as a soldier," concluded Sam.

"I can attest to that," commented Tom.

"Sam, your record of saves and rescues probably are close to that number as well, just another viewpoint," concluded Tom.

Sam thought for a moment, "Well, maybe so... Never counted... Just glad I could help out my comrades."

Sam continued, "Speaking of a couple of highlights following Vietnam, there is one other somewhat interesting story about you and me following the war that I think they should hear."

"You might want to get another tape Will," said Tom.

"Wait a minute you three", said Mae. "How about some coffee and dessert? That's a lot to take in on one night."

CHAPTER 4

THERE'S MORE?

Mae slid her chair back, stood and started for the kitchen.

"Thanks Mae," said Sam, "but instead of coffee, I'm ready for some of your homemade wine."

"OK. Tom would you like some also?" asked Mae.

"Sure would," Tom answered.

After a few moments of silence, Mae returned with four wine glasses, "I think we can all use some of this."

Mae carefully poured all a half glass of the dark wine.

After Tom took a sip of wine, "This is very good Mae - has an almost Blueberry flavor."

"Thanks," replied Mae as she smiled. "Blueberries are quite plentiful around here."

Captain Tom, after another more contemplative sip of wine, continued, "Will, this is actually not on any record or report, but your dad and I had quite an interesting time after Vietnam."

"Sam, remember Nueva in '69? - Nueva Octopus or something like that."

"You mean, Ocotepeque?" asked Sam.

"Yeah, that's right. And, it was what, my twenty fourth birthday celebration month?"

"I believe that is correct," answered Sam.

Tom continued, "And, to the best of my memory we were <u>never</u> in Honduras or El Salvador - just a training camp some place in southern Florida."

"If that's true, why do I remember both of us limping to the 'Limpy' River as you called it"...chided Sam. They both chuckled.

"What a day... Turned in to a week!" said Tom.

"That was a close one I suppose," continued Sam. "You still have that plaque from the consulate?" he asked.

"What plaque... You mean the one that became detached from the podium which I didn't kick down the stairs?" Tom asked.

"Right again," answered Sam.

"Guess I was a little upset that our guy left the day before and didn't tell anybody," Tom continued.

"The plaque – Yeah, I've got it. Told you I was going to keep it. It's in my old trunk at home. It is a beautiful piece - all hand carved by a fellow named Gerardo Marzuca if I remember correctly," answered Tom.

"Go ahead and tell the rest of that story Captain Tom. I'll get another log on the Fire," said Sam.

Sam stood, stretched, moved to the fireplace and lifted a large log onto the fire. As the fire crackled and picked up, the room began to glow.

"Thanks Sam," said Mae rubbing her arms.

As Sam came back to the table,

"Here goes," said Tom.

"The beginning of the story is that your dad and I were on a three man team dropped off near Nueve, Honduras. Richard Kelton was the third – about six and some, 180, black guy from Detroit – graduated from Nam about the same time as we did. Anyway, we were glad to have him with us.

Our mission was to get our Ambassador out of harm's way. It seemed there was some local unrest, his compound had been attacked, he'd been threatened and there was severe trouble brewing between the two countries I mentioned.

We'd had an easy time getting in it seemed. After our drop off, we had a two day jog and then simply came in through the back door of the theater so to speak," explained Tom.

It was the middle of the night and after slipping through some suburbia and around a couple of city buildings, we arrived at the rear wall of the Embassy compound.

The compound seemed pretty quiet with no guards in view. Rich quietly climbed up a small tree and was providing cover for us from atop the courtyard wall. Your dad and I climbed up and slipped over the wall and dropped into the dark courtyard.

We'd quietly but quickly crossed the grounds with no problem, but as we proceeded around the corner of the main building,"

"Dobermans," said Tom as he pulled up his left sleeve revealing a scarred bicep. Then he pointed to his scarred left hand.

Sam broke in, "Luckily they didn't bark much and I remember what you said Tom as I was taping up that ugly bleeding bicep... "Boy... that was quick. Where'd they come from?"

"And... I imagine that's what both dogs thought as they hit the ground for the last time," concluded Tom.

"Knives," Tom and Sam stated simultaneously, "They <u>were</u> enemy dogs."

"We entered the building through a side window, searched the lower basement level first then worked our way upstairs to the main level and found nobody home at all," said Tom.

"Yeah, I knew you were in a bad mood when, as we were about to head out, you spied the speakers platform and gave me that look," Sam continued.

"You just lost your temper, kicked over the podium.

Then, the United States of America plaque flew off, rolled down the stairs and hit the front door," continued Sam.

"You said, - Can't leave that piece of America behind - as you slipped down the stairs."

"Yeah... Threw it in my backpack and headed back up," said Tom.

"You know, we might have quietly disappeared that night, except for that," said Sam.

"You're probably right Sam. But how did we know there were Salvadorian troops right outside the front door? And,

Do you think Ops knew Honduras had already been invaded before they sent us in?" asked Tom.

"All I know is that we were lucky to get out of the building and extremely lucky to get out of the country. We were not supposed to be in either country," said Sam.

Tom gestured to Will, "Well the troops kicked the door in and started shooting at us. We had to return fire of course."

"Return fire?" exclaimed Sam, "There must have been 15 or 20 heavily armed troops that came through that front door just riddling the place with bullet holes. However, I do remember most of them dove for cover when we let loose."

"Well, they should have backed off further. If I remember correctly, the entire front wall fell down on them when you introduced them to the grenade launcher... Got pretty quiet for a bit," said Tom.

"We managed to slip out the back the same way we came in and were suddenly face to face with Rich in the garden. He signaled for us to follow him which we did. He'd found a drain pipe cover, that he'd already removed, let us go first, then dropped in and reapplied the cover.

"Troops surrounding the compound," he whispered. "I believe they're Salvadorian."

We crawled out the pipe and found ourselves at the edge of a pond, then quietly swam to the other side, climbed up an embankment and found some thick cover. Then we observed possibly 40 or 50 troops with flashlights combing the forest on the other side of the pond.

We silently slipped away and made it through some more of the darkened city and finally blended back into the trees at the edge of town.

Shortly after entering the forest, we got the message out that our primary extraction point planned closer to town was hot and we were headed to our secondary extraction point without the Ambassador.

"Well, to make a short story long...we had a heck of a time for a couple of days - Lots of fighting going on in the country."

Sam interjected, "At one point, we estimated the entire El Salvador Air Force was after us."

"Yeah, never dreamed I'd be shot at by a P-51... Sure sounded good though," Tom answered.

Sam continued, "What'd we do? We were just caught in the middle of something bigger than we were. They didn't know who we were, just that we were there."

Tom took over again, "Anyway, there's some background for the rest of the story."

As Tom looked over at Sam, "You might need to help me out in getting through this segment."

"Yeah I suppose. Your psychological wellbeing was somewhat questionable at that time I would say," answered Sam.

Chapter 5

MEN WITHOUT A COUNTRY

Sam began, "I'll start out on that hillside where we'd decided to catch a nap."

"We were only two or three hours from our secondary extraction point and thought our pursuers had given up on us. We hadn't heard anything the entire day."

***

"Tom! Tom! Wake up! Wake up!" exclaimed Pete.

Captain Tom began to wake up as he was being shaken by Pete.

He heard the sharp crackle of more gunfire.

"Pete, how'd they get so close?" Tom questioned.

"Tom! Tom! Wake up..." It's Sam, Sam! You've been dreaming again."

"Pete? What are you doing here?"

"Don't you remember? Come on Tom! Pete was killed in Viet Nam!" Sam frustratingly exclaimed.

"No he wasn't. He's okay!" said Tom groggily.

"He's dead Tom. It's a miracle you weren't killed as well. Don't you remember that round that hit you in the back, knocked you forward. Well, I never told you, but that round had passed through Pete's chest just before he jumped on the grenade."

After visualizing it for a sobering moment... a large tear formed in the corner of Tom's eye as he let out an anguished cry... then rubbed his hands over his eyes. As he shook off the pain and remnants of sleep, the realization had set in – again.

"Come on Tom! Those guys are really getting close!" Sam exclaimed.

Rich was quickly gathering weapons and ammo.

"Sorry Sam. Who are they shooting at?" Tom questioned.

"Remember your old hat trick?" asked Sam.

"Oh yeah." answered Tom.

"Thanks Sam," as Tom took over the tale.

"It was then I remembered, I had placed my hat with two bullet holes in it already, on a board by an old shack, stuffed some grass in it, stood it up and left it peeking around a tree about a hundred yards back."

Suddenly, there was an explosion from down the hill.

"Did one of you accidentally leave a grenade under my hat?" Tom asked as they were quickly throwing their gear together.

"Sounds like they found it," said Sam.

"Let's rock and roll," said Tom as they all grabbed the last of their gear.

"Yep, they're a little closer than I thought," Sam remarked. Then he observed Tom standing, looking down the hill, "You know Tom, I think your hat's been killed twice on this trip. Now it's blown up. Although I know you're thinking about it, it's probably not worth going back for at this time," humored Sam.

"You're probably right about that one. That's the second hat I've lost. The first, I'm told, is sitting in the MCB

Three Museum's Hall of Fame in Port Hueneme', California. It's my Beret cut to shreds by my own hand... just a prank between comrades in arms. I was disgusted but couldn't help but laugh at myself."

"You guys are crazy," remarked Rich as they moved out at a fast clip on toward the LZ.

"How'd they get so close in one night?" asked Sam.

"Don't know why they're so mad;" said Tom, "We just stumbled into their war. Now both sides are after us."

"They're probably mad because they were shooting at us with rifles across the valley and couldn't get close and you turned around and picked off two of them with your .45 ACP," answered Sam.

"They shouldn't have taken those long shots at us... L Z's about a mile ahead. Let's pick it up," Tom whispered loudly.

As they approached the apex of the hill, light began to filter through the thick foliage.

"Must be an opening ahead," said Tom.

***

Approaching a more sparsely treed area, they heard the familiar thumping sound of a Huey helicopter approaching. Rich threw a smoke canister over to a clearing indicating a suitable landing spot.

Then, they ran to a small gully for a better defensive position anticipating that the enemy troops would also hear the helicopter and show up shortly.

Suddenly from over the ridge came the black, low-flying Huey gunship.

The helicopter dropped down toward them with doors sliding open.

They ran toward the helicopter.

Suddenly the tree line behind them came alive with gunfire.

"Let's get this bird in the air!" as they all scrambled aboard.

The gunner moved back into the doorway and began blasting away with his bungeed M60 machine gun.

The helicopter began to lift off – more small arms fire, then a couple of heavier hits.

At 40 feet they had just started the takeoff turn, then … "Blam!" as the tail rotor took a hit and began spooling down.

The Pilot exclaimed, "We're not going anywhere but back down there guys…. Hang On!"

***

Back at the kitchen table in the present...

Captain Tom gestured with Mae and Will watching wide-eyed, "I'd pulled my .45," as he held up his right hand in simulation, "and was hanging on with one hand when our Machine Gunner took a hit and fell toward the open door. As I reached with my left hand to catch the Gunner, a glancing round hit my gun hand."

He showed them the scar – then, "yeeohh!" as he quickly jerked his hand back... startling both.

"I still had the Gunner by his collar," as he gestured grasping with his left arm extended, "managed to tighten up his harness, then held on for our wild ride down."

Sam chuckled, "Told you he was a good story teller."

***

"They shot my .45!" Tom yelled, as his revered pistol was knocked from his hand by the glancing round.

He held on to the Gunner in their short spiral downward. In their three turns down the Gunner never took his finger off the trigger and managed to send out another hundred rounds.

Just before touchdown, Tom spotted his Pistol and was concerned that it was not going to fire should he be able to get to it. He'd estimated his only weapon at this point had fallen at least 30, maybe 40 feet onto solid rock.

That view was short lived as the helicopter plummeted to the ground and crashed onto the same rocks.

As the helicopter contacted, it began rolling to its side with rotor blades thrashing on the rocks. The crew had done all the right things in seconds it seems as there was no fire.

As the movement stopped, there was silence for a couple of minutes. No one knew if the pursuing troops had dove for cover or if the Gunner had gotten them all.

Although the helicopter crash was violent, everyone was alive and seemingly ok. They all climbed out and dove off behind the wreckage. The Pilot had emerged with the only rifle available, an M-16, with all other weaponry buried below. The Co-Pilot scrambled out behind with the medical kit.

Captain Tom saw his pistol lying on the rocks out in the open, in front of the nose of the craft. He moved quickly, dove for it, rolled and ended up in a prone position facing where the firing had come from.

Glancing back to the others, he rose up and began to run in a low crouch toward them.

Suddenly, troops emerged from the tree line, firing and charging their position.

Not knowing if his pistol would fire, still running hard, he cocked it and let go all the rounds.

Out of the corner of his eye, he saw at least three fall, then dove for the ground, digging in his belt pack for another clip.

The rest of the troops had dropped down momentarily and then hesitatingly continued their charge.

As two rounded the front of the helicopter, the Pilot took them out with the M-16.

Then a roar came from the top of the helicopter as Sam had pulled the Sixty-Cal from its mount and lit up the area with a hail of bullets.

Then suddenly quiet.

"What? Was that it? That's all you got?" the pilot yelled as he slammed another magazine into his M16.

"Come on guys, we've got to get out of here!" Tom yelled.

Sam, "Gunny, can you walk?"

"You bet. Just a flesh wound. Let's go!" as he scrambled to his feet.

He then grabbed his bloody side and pointed, "Hey! There was a village about five clicks from here... down by the river. There were boats tied up on the bank."

They hurriedly salvaged as many weapons and as much ammo as they could find, then headed back into the thick jungle again away from their pursuers.

As they began their descent down the rugged mountain slope toward the river, it seemed they had eluded the enemy troops.

Sam, as they continued to tear through the lush mountainside foliage – again, "Tom, if we make it out of this one, let's head up to Alaska. We could get some peace and quiet. I understand it's beautiful up there - lots of wilderness. You know Jimbo went up that way about two years ago."

"Sam, can we discuss that later, just to remind you, we are ... still....running for our lives!" called back Tom.

"So.... We've always seemed to be running for our lives," Sam chided.

"And, the reason we're here... Is because..." Tom partially answered as he busted through some thick vines.

"Yeah, I remember... The day we got off the airplane back home after your recovery - San Francisco airport. You still had some shrapnel in your leg but walking ok when we ran into those creeps at the airport... and, Dang, you sure hit that one guy hard. The rest took off and we both ended up in jail in our first hour at home... That's when you made the comment that we were literally men without a country.

So..., naturally, we leave home every chance we get. We get shot at, do some running and do what we're trained to do."

"That's not the only reason we're here is it?" Tom answered as he quickly looked for an opening.

"I don't know, why don't you tell me!" Sam yelled.

"Quick, down here," Tom whispered loudly as they ducked behind the thick bushes and started on down the slope toward the river.

"Right behind you Brother!" called Sam.

"Oh no mud...mud...Mud! AAAAhhhhhhh," as both their feet dropped out from under them...slam...slice...slam as the rain soaked vines grabbed, then released... slam ...then, a clearing ahead ...both "AAAhhhh!" as they broke into a mountainside pasture, then, "Fence!!!

"Fence! Fence! Fence!" Sam yelled, then Blam!

It was hog wire, about 12 gauge with 5 inch openings. They had slammed into a non-forgiving wire net.

Now they were hanging in the fence and swaying like two climbers in a hammock on the mountainside on a windy night. All was suddenly quiet.

"Tom... you alright?" Sam asked.

Then "Creak... Creak!" as their weight settled in and began to stretch the fence to its limits. "Pop... Pop!" as staples began to pull out of the deteriorated fence posts.

"This is not good!" said Tom quietly.

Suddenly the helicopter Pilot, his Co-Pilot, Gunner Dan and Rich came crashing through the trees into the clearing,

"AAAhhhhhhhhh!"

"Crash!" as the whole fence line on the edge of the ridge began coming down, then began to break.... "Pop... Pop... Pop!" as the staples let go.

As it gave way, now out over the cliff 30 feet above the rocky ravine, suddenly, "Pop... Pop!." as the staples broke away down the line.

Then the fence came apart about 50 feet from the dangling men and like a pendulum, they all went swinging down onto the tops of the trees lining the river.

They let go once in the tree tops and plummeted through the thick trees to the muddy ground below.

The last man finally worked his way out of the tree entanglement and all were on the ground.

Laying there in silence, Tom asked, "Everyone ok?"

All checked in "okay."

"Time for intros... I'm Tom Price." "Sam Collins here." "Richard Kelton."

"I'm Captain John Roberts"... "Lieutenant David Rogers"... "Gunnery Sergeant Dan Jacobs."

Tom continued, "Great to meet you guys. Thanks for trying to get us out of there... Take a rest," as he rolled to his side, "I think we can take three minutes."

Lying there, Sam rolled to face Tom, "Hey Tom, Not to change the subject, but back to Alaska. Are there any of these steamy jungles with bad guys shooting at you up there?

"No to both, but it is cold all the time... I think," said Tom as they both rolled onto their backs looking into the holes in the trees that they made.

"Mosquitoes?" Rich asked as he crawled toward the two then slapped a mosquito on his mud covered face.

"No, I'm sure it's too cold for mosquitoes," Tom answered with a grin.

Sam glanced up at the mountainside, "Must have been at least a mile-long slide down here...Probably our record."

"At least we've got a little obstacle between us now," Tom remarked as he glanced at the mountainside.

"Look, there are the boats," called Dan as he raised and pointed then continued to crawl toward Tom and Sam.

"Come on... Let's get out of here," Tom called as he jumped to his feet.

"Tom... Probably should take all three of them," said Sam.

"You're absolutely right. We can leave two of them a couple of miles down the river," agreed Tom.

They quickly threw all their gear in and pushed off in three boats.

***

Sam and Tom drifted back to the present.

"Well, we did manage to float down the river, catch some fish, got to know the Huey crew better...turned out we were all in the Northern I Corp area during Tet," concluded Tom.

"As you can guess, we made it out as we're here now," Tom ended the tale.

"You know. I'm still not sure how we managed to stay alive through that one," said Sam.

"I believe our maker wanted to keep us around for a while," said Tom.

"Mae...Any more of that delicious wine?" asked Tom.

"Coming right up..." she answered and headed toward the kitchen.

"Thanks Mae!"

"You know Sam, I think that was about enough for both of us, especially when no one appreciated what we did out there. Heck, in general, no one even knew we were there. The guys that knew would never admit to sending us into another country on a rescue mission for a ghost hostage."

Mae brought in the wine and handed it to Sam.

"Thanks Mae," said Sam.

"You guys ready for bed?" asked Tom.

"No way..." Will answered.

"I find it hard to imagine being where you both have been."

"Of course, if I were in the same circumstances," Will continued, "I would like to think I could have done all that and be sitting here telling the stories."

"I'm very interested in how you two got to Alaska," said Mae.

"If you're sure," said Tom. "Don't want to keep you up all night."

"Please go ahead." answered Mae.

Chapter 6

COMING HOME

"Well, about 1973, we all had decided to get out of such a risky business and try civilian life for a while," began Tom.

"Every one of us went back to our home towns in Georgia, California, your dad Texas and so on."

"A few years passed during our attempt to make an adjustment into society and to live at least in or near our home towns, but... most I knew just generally didn't seem to fit in."

"As one of those 'misfits', I'd left Georgia, moved to California and eventually attained my pilot's license. While doing that, I finally finished up two years of college in only six years. As I always say, being a freshman in college was three of the best years of my life."

Mae tilted her head and looked a little puzzled... "Just joking Mae," continued Tom. "That was all night classes. I had a family now with two wonderful kids, working a full time job, attending evening classes three nights a week and flying on the weekends... kept me pretty busy."

Captain John Roberts of the crew that came to rescue us off the hill in Honduras continued to fly helicopters and was already at work in Alaska somewhere on the pipeline. His Co-pilot, Dave was also up here somewhere flying medevacs.

Our friend Jim, another Nam Man, alias Jimbo, had been in Alaska for some time and was still trying to get us all up to "The Last Frontier."

Well, he finally succeeded. By the summer of 1983, your dad and I, Rich and a few other comrades all came on up.

Dan, the Gunner in the Honduras story, had gone back home to San Antonio. He'd got his pilot's license and was flying freight into Mexico. He'd asked me to come back out West and make some real money. I turned him down more than once, thought about it, but,

Well, he did make some great money for a couple years, then one day at the Ontario, California airport shortly after clearing customs; he accidently dropped his bank roll which literally rolled between the feet of one of the Customs Agents. The agent picked up the three inch roll of hundred dollar bills and simply said, "I believe we have a little paper work to do."

He got out of that one somehow, but about six months later, he was busted just after landing his Aero Commander on a remote dirt strip in the California desert.

After doing two years in prison, he got out and now had even more adjustments to make. I think he's doing ok these days and still living somewhere near LA.

For those of us who came up to Alaska... well, we finally felt like we were home... Peaceful, quiet, no hot sweaty jungles, no mosquitoes – scratch the 'no mosquitoes' part - no hostiles, just beautiful, pristine wilderness," concluded Tom.

Sam agreed, "Yeah, it's turned out to be all we expected and more.

"Sam... You know something... I believe we both have had a better life than we've deserved," stated Tom groggily.

Mae cut in, "Ok, I think we're all getting tired now," as she slowly got up from her chair.

Tom in agreement, "You know...Probably not long until sun-up. We probably should get some sleep."

"Well, if it's sun-up you're going by, I figure you've got another seven or eight hours before getting up," chided Sam.

"Oh yeah, I forgot about that." answered Tom. "It has been a long day."

"Let's turn in." said Sam.

"Better grab a couple of extra blankets," said Will as he glanced over at the dying fire. I really appreciate you're sharing the stories."

Tom answered, "I'm glad we had this time Will. You know, you and your Mom are probably the only ones outside to hear our story. Thanks again for the nice ride over."

"Well, Good night all," said Tom as he headed toward the ladder.

"Good night. See you in the morning," answered Sam.

After climbing up the ladder into the loft, Tom found a nice comfortable bed with an old lantern sitting on the night table. He lit the lantern, then threw a couple of blankets onto the bed.

After he had stripped down to his long johns, he quickly got into bed and pulled the warm covers up under his chin. After a moment of quiet contemplation, he turned and meditated on the dancing flame in the lantern. With eyes glistening in the light it was easy to see there was a heavy feeling deep inside the man. After a moment, he leaned forward and blew out the light.

As he began to doze off, he continued to think about when he had first arrived in Alaska.

Chapter 7

ALASKA ARRIVAL - 'The First One'

'It was a cold, dark and rainy night when I and my family first arrived in the outskirts of Anchorage which I was later told was actually Eagle River, a suburb of Anchorage.

It was quite a relief to see the lights of civilization again after the long drive up.

As we entered town, we found a rather rustic hotel showing a Vacancy sign and quickly pulled into the packed parking lot.

After I'd checked in, the clerk pointed to the stairs as the direction to get to our room. I glanced up to see the rooms were set up in an atrium style just like the old western movies.

I went out to the car and proceeded to get my weary family and baggage up the stairs and into our room.

Before going in, I glanced down at the main floor again which contained a large rather antique looking bar. In the center was a dance floor, surrounded by customer tables and various game tables.

Several dart boards adorned the walls. I wasn't really sure what that was about but there were several rowdy looking folks drinking lots of beer and playing the game.

We continued into the room and settled in for the night.

As the Alaskan night progressed, the noise from downstairs continued to get louder with an occasional fist fight that would jar us awake.

Several of the guys had been wearing guns earlier and a little after midnight, we were wondering what we'd gotten ourselves into. We both agreed that we had a distinct feeling of being somewhere back in time, living in an old western movie.

Somewhere around 2 A.M., it was obvious from the banging and yelling that another fight had broken out, when suddenly, the unmistakable sound of a .38.

I quickly moved my small family over to the corner, pushed the dresser in front of them, assured them things would be ok, then cautiously left for downstairs.

It seems there'd been a fist fight and the loser had pulled a gun on the Native American victor. Robert, still standing, had been shot in the thigh and was now being held by three guys.

They struggled toward the door, then kicked the door open and threw him out into the darkness.

"Anyone call the paramedics?" I shouted as I hit the main floor.

"They're on their way," said the bartender from across the bar.

I followed the last of the crowd out the door, broke through the circle that had formed around the wounded man now writhing on the muddy ground.

I dropped to the man's side, pulled out my leather-man tool and began to cut the blood soaked jean leg looking for the bullet wound.

As I discovered the source of the blood, I began to hold pressure on the opening.

"Anyone have a blanket," I asked loudly.

"Why don't you leave him alone?" taunted a large bald bruiser who turned out to be a friend of the shooter.

"He's bleeding, got to stop it...," as I began to pull my belt off with one hand.

Suddenly from behind, he reached down, grabbed me by the neck and literally flung me up against the wall.

As he lunged forward with both hands to slam me back into the wall, my Navy days mixed martial arts response kicked in. In one motion, I grabbed both arms, slid to the side, using his own weight and momentum, banged him hard against the wall. And as he bounced off the wall, I followed with a nice hip throw to the ground.

I actually cushioned his head so as not to kill the fool as he hit the pavement. I think he weighed 230 or so.

He had no idea what had happened and couldn't get up.

Needless to say, the rest backed off.

I dropped back to my knees and applied my belt tourniquet above the wound where he was profusely bleeding. A couple of others showed up with a blanket, kneeled down and assisted as well.

As the victim began to lose consciousness, "Hello..." then he nodded off.

"Hang in there friend. The medics will be right here." I replied.

As he reopened his eyes, "Thanks. I'm Robert... Robert Weston." He went out again.

Police soon arrived with the paramedics closely in trail.

As they first came toward me, some of the crowd pointed out the shooter and his accomplice who were headed toward their pickup.

They were blocked in by another car and immediately tackled and handcuffed.

The paramedics took over the patient and shortly had him in the ambulance headed to Anchorage.

I along with everyone else returned to the bar where two of the guys approached me and offered me a beer.

I remembered the wife and kids upstairs. Said I'd be right back.

I knocked our secret knock and the door was opened. The kids were still in the blocked off corner.

I settled the wife and kids down and later went back down for my cold beer. Luckily no one was killed that night.

Everything seemed perfectly normal the next day. The family was fine and seemed glad to stay in the hotel for the day while I connected with Jim, my good friend from Reno.

I found the pay phone just outside the door and gave him a call to let him know I was close to town out near Eagle River.

As the one who persuaded me to make the journey up, he continued his enthusiasm and was anxious to show me around.

He showed up about an hour later.

"Jimbo! How'n the world are you doing?" I asked enthusiastically.

"Doin' great. I'd like to grab something to eat as I had to get up before breakfast," Jim said humorously.

"Fine by me." I replied.

"Come on; take you to my favorite restaurant." Jim replied.

After a short drive, we arrived at 'his' restaurant located just across the street from the runway at Merrill Field.

As we entered the door, several waitresses smiled, waved and said hello to him.

We were promptly seated at a booth which he mentioned was his.

Once seated, he began to harass the waitresses, joking around in his deep southern drawl. They, of course, gave it right back.

He would just smile.

During our meal, we talked about our days in Reno, college days in Atlanta, the Varsity, our trip up, and he of course briefed me on what was to come.

Toward the end of our gargantuan breakfast, as our waitress, with tray in hand, hurriedly walked past our table, "Hey Honey, you got change for a dime?" questioned Jim in a serious manner.

She quickly came to a halt.

"Why the heck do you want change for a dime Jim? That's just plain stupid," she said in a frustrated tone.

"Well, Honey," as he rolled the dime back and forth, then glanced up without moving his head ... "I really wanted to leave you a tip today," Jim answered solemnly... all in fun.

"Here's a tip for you," as she shifted her tray and raised her hand in a somewhat obscene gesture.

"Well, Tom, you ready to meet George?" as he shuffled through his wallet and then dropped a ten on the table.

"You bet I am! Thanks for that great breakfast Jim!" I paused... "However, you know, first, I'd like to drift by Providence hospital and check on the Native American fellow I helped out last night. Robert Weston was the name he gave just before he passed out. Wasn't sure he was going to make it."

"Sure, but I don't think he would be at Providence. You said he was Native American so I believe we should check the Native Hospital first," answered Jim.

After a short drive, we arrived at the hospital and were directed to the third floor and Robert's room.

After wandering around a bit, we found his room and caught the doctor just coming out.

"How's Robert Doc?" asked Tom.

"He's recovering well. The bullet missed the bone and exited the other side of his leg," answered the doctor.

"Thanks doc." replied Tom.

"Are you the fellow that applied the tourniquet?" the doctor asked.

Yes, I sure am," replied Tom.

"Well, you saved this man's life. He would have bled to death in about five minutes. The bullet clipped an artery on its way through.

"Here's your belt by the way," as he reached over and grabbed the belt off an adjacent stretcher. Sorry we couldn't get all the blood off. Robert says you're Cherokee or Creek and blood brothers anyway and that you wouldn't mind."

"He's right. Thank you doctor. Ok to look in?" Tom asked.

"Sure," answered the doctor.

Tom and Jim stuck their head in the door. Robert had fallen sound asleep.

"Looks like he needs to rest, "Tom said.

Jim agreed, "Yeah, better let him sleep."

"Ready to head to the airport?" Jim asked.

Tom gestured, "Let's go."

As we approached the sea of airplanes at Merrill Field, "Jim, I've not seen this many aircraft at one spot in my life!"

"Well, not many highways out there. These planes are our lifelines to homes and villages scattered all over Alaska," said Jim.

After driving up and down lane after lane of aircraft of every description, we pulled up to the Jordon's Aviation Hanger. I grabbed my folder with my pilot history, license and medical and we went looking for George.

George Strait, 'without the guitar,' was a tall swaggering Texan, who was quite impressive to be around. There was no doubt he was the boss, the leader of a very large Alaskan bush flying company. His fleet consisted of aircraft of all types, both fixed wing and helicopters. Everywhere I looked, I saw strong individuals taking care of business. The guys were serious about their work, yet relaxed. They were loading, unloading, fueling and performing maintenance. Others were simply cleaning up for the next flight. Two guys, obviously pilots, were doing preflight checks on their aircraft for the next trip. I was reminded of a place and time not so long ago, that is, the flight lines in Vietnam.

Many of his guys were hard core bush pilots, who would and could go anywhere and do anything within reason. These guys knew a lot and I wanted to learn as much as possible from them.

I immediately liked George and was impressed by his operation. He quickly introduced me to some of his pilots. The Chief Pilot, 'Red' Kauffman, was assigned to give me an intro to the world of Alaska aviation and to see how I flew.

I worked directly with 'Red' for a time where I learned a lot as well as had some eye opening experiences.

A few days later, I met George on the ramp where he motioned for me to follow him, "C'mon Tom. We're planning to haul some salmon over from Tyonek for the Anchorage Cannery."

As if he knew the question I was about to ask as we approached the single engine aircraft, he continued, "Tyonek is only about 50 miles from here. We're using the Cessna 206 today, somewhat of a scouting mission. We can get in and out with a few hundred feet of decent runway. With 300 horses and the high wing, it's one of the best bush planes out there. If we get an agreement with the village elders today, we'll be using the Beechcraft Queen Air to haul the fish."

***

Tom continued to relax in his comfortable bed, "Don't care to haul any more fish," he said softly to himself, then fell into a sound sleep.

...Zzzzzzzzzzzzzzzzzz

CHAPTER 8

HOW THIS TRIP GOT STARTED

Zzzzzzzzzzz...

Captain Tom was awakened by a buzz from his satellite cell phone. As he awoke, he shut off the alarm, leaned toward the window by his bed and pulled back the blackout curtain slightly, squinting, "Yea, just breaking daylight."

He tucked the curtain back to block most of the light then sat up and swung his feet onto the floor.

"As always, when my feet hit the floor in the morning, I thank You Lord for giving me another day of health, wisdom and the opportunity to improve and to help others according to Your Will," Tom prayed quietly.

"Oh boy... Here we go... Sam's not going to like this... yet another life challenging event," he mumbled to himself and began the task of getting dressed for an Alaskan winter morning.

As he carefully started down the ladder, he noticed the nice fire going in the large stone fireplace at the end of the open great room.

He paused a moment, smelled and took in the aroma of the excellent hot coffee brewing on the stove. From his lofty perch he looked around at the wonderful warm home that

Sam and Mae had put together. He slightly shook his head, then slowly continued on down the ladder.

Once down, he stretched a bit, then walked over to the table, found a waiting cup, sauntered over to the stove and poured himself some of that morning wake up brew.

After smelling the aroma of his cup, he took a sip, then drifted over toward the warm, cozy fireplace.

After warming himself for a minute, he turned around and was surprised to see through the window, Sam stepping up onto the porch.

As Sam entered the warmth of the house, "Hey... Good Morning Captain."

"Good morning Sam, You make this coffee?" Tom replied.

"Sure did. How is it?" asked Sam.

"About the best I've ever had I guess," answered Tom as he turned a little and glanced toward the fire. He could see Sam was looking at him and trying to catch his eye.

"Grab a seat Tom," as he pointed to the two rocking chairs sitting by the fireplace.

As Tom eased back and sat down in the close by rocking chair, Sam stepped forward and sat in the chair next to him.

Sam caught his eye and asked, "You know Captain, now that we've had this wonderful reunion and all, got to talk about all the warm and fuzzy stuff like Vietnam and Central America, coming to Alaska and all....., is there another reason why you're all the way out here?"

"Well Sam, thought I'd wait till this morning when I knew us two early birds would be alone. Looks like we never got out of the habit of getting up early," said Tom.

"Yeah... I knew something was up," stated Sam.

He continued, "Well Sam, seems like there may be some problems up in northwest Alaska.

"I got a call from a friend up in Holy Cross that said her brother had disappeared. And, when I discussed the situation with the Alaska State Troopers, they had nothing. They did say however, that there were several more people reported missing up in the same part of the country in recent months. That situation includes two aircraft with several passengers aboard that simply disappeared."

"The Troopers gave me the name of a fellow who might have some information and could possibly help out. I called and after a few phone conversations, met up with him in California, then one thing to another, which I'll explain more about later, here I am, back in Alaska sitting here with my number one comrade."

"Uh huh," Sam commented as he rubbed his chin.

"My deduction is that there's a group of trouble makers or possibly some kind of outside influence in more than one location north of the Alaska Range. It's quite unusual for these folks to disappear, as you know, they are a very hardy people and in general really look out for their own.

"You're right about that," replied Sam.

"You know Tom," continued Sam, "Now that we're discussing some of this; we've heard reports this year from musher's coming by that there's more folks with alcohol problems lately. No one's sure about where they're getting it or who their getting it from."

"Yeah, I know. Alcohol can be the cause of many, many problems out here," answered Tom.

"Now that I think about it, about a year ago," continued Sam, "two troopers came by, heading up river, said there were a couple of folks that went missing out of Nikolai.

Kinda suspicious, but everyone figured boat wrecks or bears."

"You know Sam, things have happened out here through the years and if you sped up the timeline, you would think we were at war... with whom I don't know."

"Just before I left for the states, when was that - about '94, I had an incident up in Wales where some folks tried to kill me and my passengers.

My folks aboard were either Federal or State, don't remember. Well, that never got resolved."

"Oh I remember," said Sam. "They'd built a three foot berm across the center of the runway and disguised it to make it disappear.

You were in Security's Conquest if I'm not mistaken.

"Sure was," Tom continued, "If you remember, luckily I spotted an unusual small one line shadow... got down low and slow and managed to see the deadly berm.

Unable to land in Wales and on their insistence to get in there, I searched the charts and found them a forestry strip about 25 miles south. They wanted to land somewhere, find a phone and try to get some type of ground transport.

I landed them on the forestry strip, but if you remember, the phone in the forestry tower had been destroyed and there was not a soul around anywhere.

After a time, I managed to contact a passing Cessna 206 aircraft by radio. The pilot was happy to assist and later ferried my folks over to Wales.

From there, I never heard anything about their mission."

"The only news from the area was that there was a mysterious crash near Wales about two weeks later whereas the pilot that helped us out was killed and his aircraft totally destroyed. The NTSB report was inconclusive suggesting pilot error. Personally, I think it was payback."

"I think you're probably right about that," said Sam.

"I hate to mention this but we had a similar situation right after you left," Sam continued. "Remember Jim Dante and Walter Gibbs, C119 - Some folks tried to kill that crew."

"Someone had built a berm across their strip as well, however this one was made of rock and was snow covered, blended in extremely well."

"The first time they saw the berm, they were only 50 feet away. It took the gear out and sent the two of them careening down the mountainside in a 20 ton sled. The aircraft was totally destroyed. It had shed the wings and had the tail broken completely off.

Both pilots survived but had some cuts and bruises."

Sam chuckled and continued, "Jim made kind of a humorous comment as the two of them stood back and looked at the smoking remains of their aircraft, "Well, they say any landing that you can walk away from is a good landing. What do you think?"

"Walter just shook his head like he couldn't believe Jim had just said that."

"Jim said that after realizing what had actually happened, they both hobbled back down to the aircraft and dug out their survival equipment, including their shotgun and some extra shells."

"Eventually, they made it back up to the strip and were met by the miners who had been on their way to meet their cargo plane. The mine was two or three miles away from the landing strip. No one had any idea who could possibly have built it or when."

"And that's what you're here for, isn't it," chided Sam as he pointed a shaking finger at Tom.

"You want me to team up with you and do some poking around – right?" asked Sam.

"Yeah Sam... It's that... and a little more. I'm pulling a whole team of people together to do some flying in those areas and into the villages where these folks have disappeared, but strictly a Recon mission," answered Tom.

Sam, with a mused look on his face, sat back in his chair and questioned, as he spelled it out slowly, "R. E. C. O. N... RECON..."

"You mean, you want me," as he gestured toward himself with both hands, "to go do sit-ups, pushups, brush up on my Jujitsu, Karate, Kung Fu, Tai Kwon Do, eat some Chinese food, run morning to night up the river and back, do target practice, fly in helicopters, airplanes, go out in the bush with bears, look for bad guys, chase them through the woods, get in shoot outs and follow you...? - all the way out there? Out There?" as he pointed out the window at the falling snow.

Captain Tom cautiously nodded 'yes' with a subdued smile and tightly clamped lips.

Sam paused, looked away for a moment, then back, "Well, that's absolutely the stupidest and most totally ridiculous thing you've ever asked of me!"

He paused again, then turned away and broke into a large grin, "When do we get started?"

As he turned back around, Tom reached forward. They grasped hands in a manly hand shake.

Tom answered and began to explain, "Well, today would be a fine day if the snow showers would let up and if we can put it together.

We'll need to head back south to Anchorage to meet up with some folks. There's quite a lot of prep required and we have a fairly short time to get things done."

"I'm game. It's the slow season around here. 'It'll give us something to do," concluded Sam.

"Mae!" shouted Sam as he stood and walked toward his and Mae's bedroom, "Got to go to town this afternoon... Would you like to do some shopping in Anchorage?"

"I'm ready," said Mae. She had obviously overheard at least a portion of the conversation.

Sam stuck his head in the door and noticed she was steadily packing for an extended trip.

Mae looked up, "I wouldn't mind staying with my sister for a few days or at least until you guys get over your end of life crisis mission."

As she got back to the task of packing, "I'll get some breakfast going in a minute."

Sam smiled, ambled over and gave his wife a hug from behind, "It'll be alright. We'll just find out what's been going on, get it reported and get on back home."

Mae pulled away and moved to the window, pulled the curtain back. With glistening eyes, she stared into the flurrying snow, "After those stories last night, do you expect me to believe the two of you aren't going to find some trouble out there?"

"Tom said they want us strictly for a recon mission, nothing more," answered Sam as he approached and again hugged her from behind.

He continued, "Besides, you've wanted to get to town and catch up with your Sis."

"Guess you're right about that," Mae answered as she turned around inside his arms, "Alright... Just make sure you come back to me."

They embraced, kissed, then she reluctantly and gently pushed him away, turned and continued to pack.

Sam strolled back into the living room, "Snow's lightning up. Better get some things together myself."

"Will! You up?" as he stuck his head inside another bedroom, "Best drag out the machines... Heading over to Lime bout one o'clock. Let's hook up a sled to one of them... Need to get going... Your Mom should have breakfast here shortly."

As he re-approached Tom now standing by the fire, "By the way, Tom, there are a lot of villages to cover. Who else do you have in mind to fly with us?"

"I thought we'd discuss that and some other items on the way down to Anchorage. I've already contacted some of the guys but feel free to suggest any others you feel would best complete our team.

"Sounds good," said Sam.

"Breakfast in about 15!" sounded Mae from the kitchen.

Tom greeted Will as he sleepily walked into the room, "Good morning Will. I'll give you a hand with the snow machines when you're ready."

"Ready now," answered Will.

Tom and Will threw on their parkas and headed out the door.

Chapter 9

IN TO ANCHORAGE

Mae finished setting the table and poured four fresh cups of coffee.

She had placed a bowl of scrambled eggs, a plate of ham and a generous platter of biscuits onto the large Lazy Susan on the table.

As they sat down for breakfast, Mae asked, "Are you sure this isn't dangerous?"

"Oh heaven's no, said Tom. "We're simply the eyes and ears of an ongoing investigation. We're just going to do what we did back in the eighty's and ninety's... deliver groceries and supplies... just add take notes and call in some reports."

"Well, the weather in itself is dangerous," replied Mae.

"We'll be careful," said Sam as he reached and gently squeezed Mae's arm.

After an enjoyable breakfast, Mae and Will began to clear off the table.

Captain Tom reached into his leather backpack and pulled out a map, pointing, "The villages circled here have the most recent reports, say over the last three years."

"If you notice they're all inland but with easy access to the coast generally via the rivers - not sure if that's significant or not."

"When we get down to Anchorage, I'm going to call a friend at NASA to see if we can get some images around or between these villages and look for any interesting signs or patterns."

"Well," said Sam, "You and I both have covered all of those villages one time or the other. Back in those days we knew just about everybody that lived there by name, flew most of them in and out and brought some of them into the world on our way back to Anchorage."

"That's true, and that's partly why we've been elected to do this job," said Tom.

Both turned as Mae sat her two suitcases outside the bedroom door.

"Looks like Mae's about ready, I'll get my gear out of the barn and load up the sled," remarked Sam.

"I'll give you a hand," said Tom.

As they walked toward the barn, Sam asked quietly, "Not needing any additional weapons.... are we....?"

Tom shook his head, "negative on that."

After entering the barn, Sam walked off to the right, kicked away some straw from a section on the floor.

He smiled as he reached down, grabbed a ring and pulled up a large trap door.

He reached down and switched on the light, motioned for Tom to take a look. Tom peered down into the basement which was apparently a fully equipped armory.

"Not... right at this moment...," answered Tom.

"However, it's good to know this is here ... might need to stop in later on down the road should we need to equip a small army," continued Tom.

Sam clarified, "Don't worry. These are sanctioned Guard weapons. We just store them here. But for now, it's just a camera mission, right?"

"Yeah, that's right. And we've got all the cameras we need waiting for us in Anchorage," answered Tom.

They heard the first snow machine pull up out front, Sam shut off the light, stood and closed the trap door.

Back outside in the crisp cold air, now turning into a bright Alaskan day, they pulled the tarp from the sled, loaded and secured the bags.

After a time, Will came around with the second snow machine, shut down and together they pulled the loaded sled out and attached it.

Will, with Tom as passenger, took the lead machine and headed back down the river trail toward Lime Village. Sam, with Mae as his passenger followed pulling the sled along.

The run was uneventful but very scenic with the only stop being a pause to let a rather large Moose amble off the trail.

Tom felt he really preferred the dogsled which was much quieter and much more comfortable.

They arrived at the airstrip and began to clear off the snow and remove the covers from the Cessna 206. Will went to the shed and pulled the 'red devil' out along with the ducting.

After the aircraft was substantially heated, with bags stowed, all but Will climbed aboard.

The window open, Sam called out, "Will, take care of the ranch. If you need us for any reason, use the satellite phone Tom gave you."

"Ok. See you in a couple of weeks," answered Will.

The aircraft started easily and after the chilly snow machine ride, the heated cabin felt good to all.

Captain Tom began to taxi out and lined up in takeoff position at the end of the snow covered strip.

Powering up, he taxied down to the other end of the runway, made a U-turn and taxied back to their starting point.

Mae asked, "When are we going to take off?"

Sam answered, "When the Captain's ready. He's grooving the runway so we can take off in this much snow."

Tom added, "Yeah... Had I known there would have been this much snow, I would have put on the skis."

After four circuits on the runway, "Sam, what do you think, look okay to you?" Tom was satisfied but verified with his highly experienced co-pilot.

"Let's do it," Sam replied.

The takeoff roll was short. They climbed out steeply with the 206 engine echoing throughout the river basin.

As they climbed out heading up the river, Tom lowered the wing in a right turn for Mae and Sam to get a good view of their white, snow covered ranch.

In the distance, the formidable Alaskan Range loomed ahead.

"Looks like Merrill Pass should be open, sound okay?" Tom asked Sam.

"No problem here," answered Sam.

Surrounded by the rocky, 8,000 foot, snow covered mountains they negotiated the pass easily with just a few bumps.

As they exited the pass, the pristine Kenibuna Lake appeared below followed shortly by the much larger Chakachamna Lake. Fed by glacier melting waters, they both appeared extremely cold due to the large white ice bergs floating along the center of the lake.

As they continued to follow the river, off to their left, appeared the ominous 11,000 foot Mount Spurr.

"Looks quiet today," remarked Sam, as they both gazed at the mountain.

"Yeah, I remember when it was touted as a. dormant volcano... Until that day it exploded of course. I remember there was a lifeguard crew that came close to oblivion."

"Yeah, within a couple of minutes I understand,"

"Look, there's the Sleeping Lady," remarked Mae. "Getting close to town," as she tried to ignore the conversation the mountain had produced.

As they rounded the Sleeping Lady, (Mt. Susitna), the picturesque City of Anchorage came into view.

With the afternoon sun shining, the glistening city stood, like a jewel of civilization, with the waters of the Cook Inlet as a foreground and the snow covered Chugach Mountains as a backdrop.

"How beautiful," Mae remarked.

"Very nice today," Sam agreed as he smiled and touched Mae's arm.

"Our flight down has been uneventful and spectacular as well... just like we like them to be," confirmed Tom.

Tom checked in with Anchorage approach, "Anchorage approach, this is N714JP, Sleeping Lady, with Alpha, landing Anchorage International."

"Roger, N714JP - Runway Seven Left. Turn right to one three zero degrees for spacing," directed the controller.

When he had a break in communications, Sam asked, "Tom, quick question, we've got several weapons aboard - Didn't know we were landing at International."

Tom dug into his shirt pocket, "Here's your I.D. Card with permission to carry. You're working as a Federal Agent now."

"Well, that was pretty presumptuous of you and the U.S. Government I haven't signed anything yet," stated Sam.

I knew you would come along so I signed for you," stated Tom.

Sam shook his head in disbelief, "Ok Captain. Glad you were thinking ahead."

They landed at Anchorage International and taxied toward a group of non-descript hangars.

As they arrived on the parking ramp, Tom pulled back the mixture killing the engine. As he completed his shutdown checklist, an SUV with three linemen aboard, pulled up beside the aircraft.

The men hurriedly exited their vehicle and were standing by to unload the aircraft.

Tom, as they got out of the aircraft, "Sam, Mae's bags can go into the SUV. We should take ours into the hangar with us. Not sure where we go from here, but I believe we have rooms at one of the hotels."

After the aircraft was unloaded, the tug was hooked on and the aircraft was pulled inside the hangar.

"Mae, will you be ok to head over to Julie's by yourself, "asked Sam. "Tom said we had a meeting here shortly. We can catch up this evening."

"No problem, I know my way from here," answered Mae.

Tom approached, "Mae, this is your vehicle for the duration of our mission."

"Here's both our satellite phone numbers if you need anything at all," as he handed her a slip of paper and Sam his phone.

"Thanks," said Mae.

"Mae, I'll be seeing you in a couple of hours," said Sam.

Both Tom and Sam stood in silence at the gate and watched her drive away.

A quick glance at each other and they turned and began walking toward the hangar. Both seemed to have an old feeling come alive.

"Tom, why do I feel we're about to leave the 'world' again," Sam said quietly.

Tom answered, "Yeah, I know what you're saying. That's all a lot of guys talked about in the old war days... was what we were going to do when we get 'back to the world."

'Tom thought to himself and pictured, Bill, his radioman, Vietnam, had spoken that very statement a couple of hours before we got to the rice patty - Seems like he was going to start a car restoration business - "When I get back to the world..."'

They both continued to walk in silence. Both chose not to bring up any of the thoughts flooding their minds.

Chapter 10

THE COLONEL

Tom and Sam entered the side door of the hangar as directed by the linemen, then found themselves in a corridor hosting several offices, all with combination codes to enter.

As Captain Tom reached for the nearest door knob, the door quickly inwardly swung open. A sharp looking military type, armed with a side arm had opened the door and in sharp attention, "Hello gentlemen, I'll see if the Colonel is available."

He picked up the phone, pressed the number, spoke with someone quietly.

As he hung up the phone, "Follow me gentlemen. You can drop your bags right over there in the corner - We're in a secure area. He's over in the Charlie hangar - quite a distance - Said to bring you over."

Both had reached for their wallets for I.D. but were interrupted by the guard, "Sirs, we're ok on identification. We have an electronic means."

They dropped their bags into the corner looked at each other, then followed the obvious security man to the rear of the first hangar and out the door, then through another coded door into another very large hangar.

Quite noticeable were the two well-armed, dark green Huey helicopters in the center of the hangar and that along the walls were racks holding various types of weaponry including several missiles.

Tom and Sam glanced at each other.

They continued to follow the guard and as they rounded one of the helicopters, there, working in a sweat shirt and jeans was the Colonel.

The Colonel turned around wiping a greasy wrench in his hand, reached and laid it on the table.

Tom guessed the Colonel was about 50, slightly gray, well-built and obviously in excellent condition.

Both almost saluted but remembered they were civilians. They reached out and shook hands with the Colonel.

"Glad to finally meet you Tom, Sam. Heard a lot about you both," said the Colonel.

He motioned and they headed toward an office at the rear of the hangar. As he could see, Tom and Sam were carefully scrutinizing the operation.

"Kind of impressive for a civilian outfit huh?" asked the Colonel.

"Quite impressive Colonel," remarked Sam.

As the Colonel entered the office, "Have a seat," then reached into an adjacent file cabinet. After searching for a moment, he pulled out a thick file, turned and sat down with them.

The Colonel introduced himself, "My name's Colonel William Talbot, just call me 'Bill' if you don't mind at this juncture.

He was about to continue when Tom interrupted, "Before we get started Colonel, just curious about your electronic identification process. Were we scanned or something?"

"Yes you were... We have F R S here. They locked on to you when you exited your aircraft," answered the Colonel.

"Here we go Sam, another T L A do deal with," stated Tom.

Sam shook his head.

After a thoughtful moment, the Colonel questioned, "Ok... What is a T L A?"

"I'll tell you when you tell me what an F R S is," answered Tom.

"F R S - Facial Recognition System," answered the Colonel.

"T L A - Three Letter Acronym," answered Tom.

The Colonel thought for a minute, then half smiled and continued to explain, "What you've seen here so far is simply back up for the Anchorage P.D., State Troopers, or even the guard. The concern is they may be outgunned here at some point by some of the folks hanging around or living out on the fringes of civilization."

"You don't say?" commented Tom as he remembered the armory under Sam's barn.

"Tom, as we discussed several times on the phone, we really need some people on the inside which as you probably know can be a tricky proposition."

"We've already sent in several agents. Two have totally disappeared. We're not sure if they overstepped their boundaries with the locals or if there's another more sinister force at work."

"Where you come in... We need someone that can come and go and fit into the normal bush lifestyle. Then to find out who, what, when, where and why for us - strictly Recon."

"The idea to send in pilot-agents in bush aircraft came out of our last meeting. You'll be more mobile and can provide eyes and ears for us and be generally accepted by the locals. The mission so far has gone on for nine weeks with zero results except for the two missing agents."

"Even our elite State Troopers are perplexed at that as well as the increase of drugs and alcohol intercepts in the last six months."

He turned to a map of Northwest Alaska, "We still do not know what's wrong up there."

He pointed to a shaded area between the Alaska Range and the northwestern Alaska Coast, "As you can see, there are about 25 villages scattered throughout this area. At this point, we have confirmed at least 19 folks have gone missing from here this year."

"I know you'll probably request a NASA satellite photo study, however, we've been in the process for several weeks and not found any anomalies," stated the Colonel.

"With that in mind, and after much discussion, we feel someone is needed to mix in with the day to day life out there. And, we believe you and your team concept is the right choice to help us get the best result."

"And Bill, who are 'we'?" asked Tom.

"That's top secret of course, however, you both had top secret clearances in the military, and you do now, so I can at least tell you this."

"For this project, you have all the assets of every branch of the military available to you with one call from your satellite phone."

"Wow," commented Sam.

"Tom, what's the status of the rest of your pilots?" the Colonel asked.

"Two are already here in Anchorage. The rest are coming in later today," answered Tom.

The Colonel continued, "From the resumes' I've read, all of you have shown you can handle Alaska's natural traits. As you know, she's beautiful but can be deadly at the same time. An added plus is that you all know a lot of the folks in the villages already."

"I agree. I believe we have the right guys to get the job done for sure," answered Tom.

"That all sounds fine Colonel - Bill, sorry... but how are we going to compete with the incumbent companies," asked Sam.

"Well, we're asking two of the airline and airfreight operators to stand down for an FAA maintenance type investigation. Our fill-in company aircraft will be picking up several of their routes.

"Probably be accepted," commented Sam.

"Tom, you are in command of the mission in the field. Sam, you are the backup in case Tom is down for any reason," continued Bill.

"You mean if I oversleep or have a flat tire on the way to work or something, right?" asked Tom.

The Colonel with an unchanging expression, "You've got me twenty four hours a day, seven days a week."

He picked up his papers, rearranged them and shut his folder.

"Tom, Sam, we know you both have some history in the military, Navy and Army primarily, but have worked with Marines and the Air Force, some black ops down south, and most of all, you both have a ton of Alaska experience."

"<u>However</u>, this is possibly different; no, I'll say this is probably going to be quite a different experience for you both."

"We believe there is a sinister element in or nearby several of the villages, especially from Bethel north and possibly eastward as well."

"We're going to supply you with whatever you need, including aircraft. If you accidentally wreck it beyond repair, we'll get you a new one."

"Again, your mission is strictly Recon and we expect only safe and conservative actions on your part," he concluded.

"Sounds good," concluded Tom.

As they stood to exit, "C'mon, I'll give you a quick tour of some additional assets you have at your disposal."

Tom and Sam followed now 'Colonel Bill' out a door from the Briefing Room and entered another even larger hangar.

As they walked inside, visible to them were eight or nine Cessna 206's, which all appeared to need paint. Down at the end of the long line of Cessna's sat a Super DC-3 with very poor paint as well. There were several mechanics working on the aircraft.

"Gentlemen, this is our bush aircraft refurbishment shop... Pretty rough huh?" the Colonel asked.

Sam looked at Tom, "How much are we getting paid again?"

"Don't be deceived... These are not your ordinary aircraft," the Colonel interceded.

He pointed at the hangar door and moved his hands together, signaling the door to close. The huge doors closed rapidly.

Again, Tom and Sam looked at each other.

The Colonel continued, "We're watched constantly here by security cameras. I like to check occasionally to see if my boys are paying attention."

They approached the first Cessna 206 whereas Bill opened the door on the pilot's side. He motioned for them to take a look inside. As they got closer, he walked around the tail to the right side of the aircraft and opened the passenger side door.

Then, as he glanced over his shoulder, he placed his right fist into his left palm signaling a nearby mechanic to plug in the ground power unit.

The mechanic plugged it in and gave him a thumbs up.

As they studied the somewhat rough cockpit area, "Tom, flip on the master and avionics switch," asked the Colonel.

Tom positioned the master on, then the avionics.

As they both watched, the gyros began spinning up and the standard Cessna radios slowly came alive.

"Pretty impressive right?" said the Colonel finally with a slight smile as he watched their expressions.

"So far, seems like seventy's technology - nice color though," answered Tom glancing down and scratching his left cheek, withholding a chuckle.

The Colonel continued, "Check this out as he stretched and reached across to the left side panel.

"If you notice," he ran his finger under the panel, "there's a small switch about here." He flipped it on.

The left front panel disconnected and began to slide down and forward out toward the firewall, revealing a state of the art G3000 panel.

"So... We have two working sets of instruments, round gauges or the latest and greatest avionics technology," stated Tom.

"That's correct. I know you don't recognize these aircraft as brand new, but they came straight out of the factory and over to Avionics. Then we brought them up here where we applied our own paint with 70's and 80's paint schemes. As you can tell, we changed out the interiors as well - all part of the cover."

Sam began turning knobs and pushing buttons watching the screen reveal continuous volumes of information.

"So, if we want to watch TV, we push that button," Sam chuckled as he pointed at the under panel button.

The war-wise Colonel didn't smile, "The first thing we're going to do is get all of you trained on the avionics and equipment over the next couple of weeks."

"I know you all have hundreds of hours in the Cessna 206 aircraft as well, however, this is not a standard 206."

"There are three major differences. One is that you have dual NiCad batteries with a small back up lead acid."

"The other is that to compensate for the approximate 167 lbs. of equipment and steel plated doors and bulletproof windows, we added an ungoverned 450 horse power IO-580 Lycoming engine."

"If you notice on the throttle quadrant," he pointed to the levers on the console, "you've got one more detent to get to max power.

"From the full throttle position, move it to the left side then forward to whatever you need. You'll have total ungoverned full power for the engine. It will feel like a JATO bottle and is designed to get you out of a tough spot if necessary. There's a five minute time limit on the JATO System Power, we'll call it, simply for clarity. The timer automatically appears on your G3000 screen as soon as you push it forward."

"Last, but not least, you have both electric and manual flaps..., And, as you can see, the manual flap handle here..." as he pointed between the seats, "has a release button to disengage the electric motor. This enables you to immediately set a needed flap setting to pop off a rough strip or to dump flaps immediately in a high cross wind landing."

"Tom, I believe that was one of your first requests to Cessna engineering," concluded the Colonel as he glanced up at Tom.

"Sure was," answered Tom.

"Now that's remarkable. New aircraft, latest technology, bush friendly, and comes with a super thrust engine," Sam said.

"How about Communications?" asked Sam, "When we're out there, even with satellite phones, there can be communication problems."

"Come with me," said the Colonel as he gestured for them to follow.

They went past the other 206's and walked up to the large Super DC3.

"I don't have to tell you what this is," continued the Colonel as they walked under the wing of the somewhat beat up looking Super DC 3. "This is 'Mother.' She's not what she appears to be."

"Old cargo bird right?" Asked Sam.

"Well, that's the way it appears from the outside," answered the Colonel.

As they pulled open the large cargo door, oil drums, tires and boxes just about blocked the door making it appear to be really packed to the gills.

"Not sure if the FAA would like this..." said Tom as he glanced at the drum partially blocking the doorway.

The Colonel smiled, turned and motioned the fist in the palm signal again.

"Come on in," he nodded and motioned for them to follow, then turned and squeezed between the fake oil drums.

Once inside, "From here everything changes," as he pressed a code into a small pad beside a forward secondary entry door.

The heavy door opened. "Here you go..." stated the Colonel as everyone began to follow him inside. The lights came on and the room came alive with obviously state of the art radar and communication panels.

The right side wall of the room featured three large 'glass' panels. To the left was another two with one an obvious targeting panel. Both sides had three chairs each for personnel to operate and monitor.

"As you can see... Not your normal DC3," the Colonel said proudly.

"With satellite communications, real time terrain and obstacles and with multi-faceted tracking capabilities, we can monitor your every move. We will know where all your aircraft and ours are at any given time anywhere in Alaska."

Both Tom and Sam were impressed to see such a state of the art Command Center.

"This reminds me of our 'Spooky' or Puff the Magic Dragon during the Vietnam Era," said Sam.

"Speaking of that," the Colonel stepped closer to the cockpit door and turned to the left couch and window.

"Hey, I didn't see a window from the outside," remarked Sam.

"Nice what camouflage can do isn't it," answered the Colonel.

"This is a one-way window. We can see through it but it appears to be solid from the outside. It's designed for night operations as well with green light as well as infrared capabilities. As he pressed a toggle switch on the panel, "Kill the hangar lights please."

As the lights died down, from their concealed cabin, in a pale green atmosphere, the men could still see everything, including details of the mechanics clothing.

"Watch this," as he selected Infrared.

Anything producing heat was brightly illuminated.

Another "Wow," came from Sam.

He pushed an adjacent button on the right side of the panel which separated and retracted into the lower section of the aircraft side wall. His display screen reverted all to the half panel.

Standing and stepping aside, he pulled down a large lever next to the window, the chair slid backwards; the floor opened exposing a large state of the art dual Gatling gun system.

He touched another button on the console, whereas the guns laying parallel to the floor rose up hydraulically, pivoted and extended outward through a previously unseen opening.

They could see on the reverted screen, all the men moving to each side out of any possible alignment with the deadly guns.

The Colonel pushed another button and the process reversed and the guns stowed automatically.

"That's not all," continued the Colonel, as he stepped back toward the rear of the cabin. As he bent down and opened a hatch on the floor, "We've got six missiles mounted on this turret in the floor that we can turn in any direction for launch."

As the hatch fully opened up, the tops of the missiles came into view, "I believe we can cover your backs in case there's trouble."

"Seems like an awful lot of protection for a photo mission," chided Tom.

The Colonel didn't crack a smile and continued, "Defensively, most of our additional weight on this aircraft is in the reinforced skin."

"Unlike your 206, we have a pair of actual JATO bottles in the tail," as he pointed aft.

"Our Armory is in here," as he turned and opened another sliding door revealing several types of the latest automatic weapons, grenades and other explosives.

"Plus," as he opened another compartment door on the right side and forward, "we have an on-board clinic with a doctor aboard on every flight."

"Now that's good to know... in case one of us gets a migraine... or something." Tom humorously interjected.

The Colonel ignored the comment, turned and pointed to the front bulkhead, "The red wall phone has a direct line to our military coordinator should we feel they're needed."

He pressed the toggle switch on the panel, "Hangar lights up please."

As they finished the tour and stepped down out of the aircraft, the Colonel continued, "I'd like to give you 48 hours to get your guys together, take care of any unfinished business and report back here to the briefing room at 0800 Saturday morning... Sorry about the start date but that's the only open class they had available."

"No problem here," answered Tom.

"It will be okay to give your guys a briefing to cover what we've discussed and what you've seen today prior to their coming here," continued the Colonel.

"As soon as you get your guys together, we'll schedule you to get started on G3000 School up in Galena, just to get you up to date on the new avionics and communication package. They've got state of the art simulators that can be adjusted to any aircraft."

"That sounds good Bill," answered Tom

"Say, Colonel Bill, is there any suspicion of Russian activities? ... Just curious," asked Tom.

"There's absolutely no evidence that points in that direction. Our preliminary investigation indicates nothing from the Russians," answered the Colonel.

As the Colonel continued to usher them toward the exit, "There'll be a golf cart outside the door to take you to your vehicles."

As he reached for the exit door knob, "Well, it's been a pleasure meeting you both. I'm really looking forward to working with you on this project."

"Ok Colonel, we'll see you Saturday," said Tom as they shook hands.

"As mentioned, you can call me Bill," stated the Colonel.

"Well, Colonel Bill ok, 'cause one of our Captain's name's Bill, might be confusing down the line," said Tom.

"OK... Colonel Bill... See you in a couple of days," replied the Colonel.

As they walked away from the building toward the parking area, Sam, rubbing his chin, "Say isn't Galena the base where the MIG flew by the tower twice and the pilot flipped them off, and then disappeared over the horizon westbound at about Mach Two."

"Yeah, but remember, that was back in the 80's before we got the new over the horizon radar net," answered Tom.

"And remember when the Cold War ended, there were only 84 Bear Bomber intercepts the next month," continued Sam.

"I do remember that... I also remember that day coming down the coast from Nome, we were somewhat in the line of fire of those three F16's that luckily ATC headed away from us," answered Tom.

"Yeah... Quite a site," said Sam as they both visualized the almost vertical flight of the three interceptors, watched them split out of formation to get around their Conquest II, then re-form at high altitude on the wings and tail of the Bear Bomber.

***

As they approached their waiting vehicles, Sam began to walk around, then scrutinize the older model SUV's, "I kinda expected something a little better than these," said Sam as they both gazed at the rusty looking vehicles.

"I guess we're waayyyy under cover - probably special engines or something," as Sam turned the ignition switch the vehicle refused to start.

"Hold the pedal down on the floor for a second or two and hit it again," answered Tom.

The engine roared to life.

"We're good," said Sam with a smile.

"I'll get the guys to meet us in the conference room of the hotel about 0900 if that sounds okay with you," said Tom.

"Sounds good... And I'll catch up with Mae; see if I've gone broke yet. See you then," replied Sam.

Chapter 11

THE 'TEAM'

After a good night's sleep and a good breakfast, Captain Tom met up with Sam and the others at the hotel conference room.

As he closed the door, he and Sam began walking around the room visiting and shaking hands.

"Jimmy... You rascal... You're the reason we all came up to Alaska the first time I suppose... Don't know if I ever formally mentioned it but thank you for being persistent and excited in your efforts... Been quite a life for all of us," greeted Tom.

Jimmy nodded and smiled.

Michael... 'Buck...,' you look good," not indicating that anything was wrong with him to the others. "You ready to do some flying with us?"

"What do you think?" answered Buck. "Good pay, airplane, and working with my friends... Yeah, I'm ready," he concluded.

'Buck,' alias, Michael Land, had been living in a Hospice in Seattle, sent there by some folks in Anchorage after the hospital had tagged him as terminal. He was fighting for his life with Giardia or 'Beaver Fever' as it's sometimes called, mixed in with several other complications.

However, after a few phone conversations, he indeed convinced me that if I could get him back to Alaska, he would live at least another year or so.

The short story was that about a year and a half ago, he dumped most of the meds being given to him daily, got dressed one morning, walked out of the Hospice facility, caught a cab to the airport and flew up to Anchorage.

Our local Baptist Church provided a decent apartment to get him started. Once he got off all the meds he'd been taking, he gradually regained some strength and realized some remission in the disease, got his medical back, and within a couple of months he was back in the air. A short time afterward, he left for the western Alaskan coast to 'get back in the bush.'

He was right. He had radically improved while in this pristine environment and eventually picked up a job flying Cessna 207's just outside of Bethel.

"Bob Reynolds... 'Bear Man'... Good to see you brother. How's the wife and the twin boys...," Tom questioned.

"All good," replied Bob.

"Let's catch up soon. I'd like to hear more about the family and maybe hear a few more bear stories."

"Sounds good Tom," he replied.

As they continued around the room, "Jerry Bagwell! - 'Bag Man!'

It's really good to see you today. You ready for a little adventure?" asked Tom as he gave the oldest member of the team a gentleman's hug.

"Captain, I was born for adventure... Let's get going," he answered.

They all took their seats and noticeably one chair was empty.

"Who's missing?" asked Tom.

"Red's missing," said Sam.

"You mean, Wild Bill. He doesn't like 'Red' anymore. Probably should drop that name," mentioned Buck.

"Anyone know if he's come up to Anchorage yet?" asked Tom

Jimmy answered, "I talked to him two days ago. He said he was going to try to get in one more rodeo before getting killed again in Alaska. He broke a couple of airplanes somewhere in the past, don't know all the details. Said he'd been shot at a few times as well,"

"And, I've got a feeling that the reason he isn't here is that he made the Bull Riding finals which are going on today," continued Jimmy as he glanced at his watch.

"How does he keep doing that?" asked Bob. "He's the same age as all of us, so how can he possibly hang on to a 2,000 pound animal that's pure muscle and has one purpose in life... to kill the person sitting on his back?"

Tom continued, "You know, 'Wild Bill' has worked the rodeo circuits just about all his life while he was flying airplanes. He's won several championships and was Rodeo Rookie of the Year in '63 when he won the bull riding championship over in Cheyenne, plus, he's qualified at least seven times for National Finals.

On top of his Rodeo and flying career, he's also a Tri-Athlete and Fitness Trainer and plans to 'live till he dies or die trying to live.'

And you guys thought you all had a busy life," concluded Tom.

Sam said quietly to Tom, "We really need that guy as you know Tom. Not only that he's one of our best, but we've got lots of territory to cover and he knows it better than any of us."

Tom thought for a minute, then looked at Sam, "You know that Lear 36A sitting on the ramp... Colonel Bill would probably let us borrow it for a few hours.

"What about our meeting?" asked Sam.

"We can continue our meeting after we pick up Wild Bill this afternoon - considering he's able to travel," concluded Tom.

"That's actually a great idea. Much more private at 35,000 feet than here," said Sam.

"Let's all go!" suggested Tom. "Haven't been on a Lear in a while - Haven't been to a rodeo in a while either."

They all picked up their materials, stuffed the donuts into their pockets and headed for the coffee maker for the cup to go.

Sam, as he traded glances with Tom and chuckled, "some things never change."

They all jumped into the two SUV's and headed for the hangar.

"Don't you think you should call ahead Tom?" asked Sam.

"Yeah," answered Tom as he thought for a second.

"Did any of you gentlemen see any kind of a bug in the hotel or conference room, even a dead one," Tom asked of the guys in his vehicle.

"As a matter of fact, I did see a dead one on the floor near the coffee service area, but that was yesterday," answered Jimmy seeming to catch the drift of things.

Tom took his new satellite phone from the pouch and pressed the number he was given for the Colonel.

"Hello, Colonel Bill," as he placed the phone on speaker. "I hate to report this but, Captain Jim was scanning the hotel conference room and found a bug. Seemed dead, probably old, but we all feel we need to have our meeting somewhere very private."

"Well, you're welcome to use our conference room here," answered the colonel.

"Not that we don't trust you guys, just like to get somewhere where we can relax and talk freely," continued Tom.

"What's the Lear 36A doing today?" as he gestured toward the ramp.

"Nothing on the schedule as far as I know," answered the Colonel.

"OK, well we've got one other problem. One of our guys, Bill Kauffman, has been delayed down in Tucson. We really need to get him here today."

"We would like to borrow the Lear and pick him up if that's possible. We could continue our meeting on the way down and on the way back. We'd like to get down there by two or three o'clock and get on back this evening."

"Sure, I'll get a crew out there right away," said the Colonel.

Tom smiled into the rearview mirror as a couple of guys high fived.

After a few minutes, the two SUV's arrived at the gate and were flagged through to their waiting aircraft where the pilots were just completing their preflight.

All seven climbed aboard and were belting in and reading the briefing cards.

"Tom, you know he'll never come up unless we hog tie him to that seat right there," said Sam as he pointed to the empty seat, "not really warm and fuzzy about the Federal Government right now."

"Yeah, I know," answered Tom.

As the door closed, the engines began to spool up.

"Might want to get some sleep on the way down - Not sure what we'll run into down in Tucson, Arizonaia," announced Tom.

Chapter 12

PICKING UP 'RED' - (I MEAN 'WILD BILL')

The high altitude flight went smoothly non-stop into Tucson.

After landing and shutdown, the men noticed the rapid approach of two black Government SUV's.

As the vehicles parked adjacent to the passenger door of the Lear, the drivers exited their vehicles and moved to greet the passengers.

As the men exited the aircraft and boarded the SUV's, Tom asked loudly, "Where's the Fairgrounds and is there a Rodeo still going on?"

The driver's looked at each other questioningly. The second driver shrugged and gestured to give them whatever they want.

"There's a Rodeo but should be just about concluding," stated the first driver as he glanced at his watch. "I think all's left would be the Bull Riding finals."

"Can you get us there right away?" asked Tom.

"Sure can. Gates should be open. I can drive you right to the stadium - about 10 minutes," answered the driver.

They took off quickly with the second SUV following.

With their lower strobes flashing, they were waved through the gate and continued toward the stadium.

Tom glanced at the situation and saw where the riders were staging.

"Can you get us around there?" as he pointed to the back of the open air stadium.

"Sure," as the two vehicles tore around to the back.

As they arrived, they all ran for and climbed onto the fence where several cowboys sat.

They immediately spotted Bill, tightening his strap on top of the bull.

Sam remarked, "Tom...That is a huge animal."

"What is that? Is that a Brahma?" yelled Jerry.

Hope he's still alive after eight seconds, Sam said quietly."

"You and me both Sam," answered Tom.

"Ladies and Gentlemen," blared over the speakers, "At Gate Number Six... Riding Tornados Extreme... Seven times National Champion! - Captain Wild Bill Kauffman!!!

Rinnnnnggggg...! The crowd was deafening as the gate swung open.

'Wild Bill' and his raging ride came storming and twisting out of the gate right in front of his long lost comrades.

"Now that's timing," shouted Jerry as he readjusted himself on the fence.

As the horn sounded, 'Wild Bill' continued to hold on for four or five more seconds, then swung his leg over and leaped away from the deadly bull. He landed on his feet, pulled off his hat and waved to the cheering crowd.

The clowns had done their job well and had lured the bull off into another direction.

As the roar of the crowd began to die down, they all headed over by his exit gate and positioned themselves.

"What the heck are you guys doing here?" asked a surprised Bill as he approached the gate.

"You're still looking pretty good out there," said Tom.

Others responded as well, "Great Ride Bill! Wow!"

"Thanks guys. My goal every day is to do today what I did yesterday, that is, if the Good Lord's willing," responded Bill.

"Same here I suppose," said Sam. "But aren't we talking 25 or 35 years of yesterdays and today's on bulls and in airplanes?"

Bill grinned and threw his gear over his shoulder and kept walking ahead, "Well, you know... experience does help."

The small group all entered into the small Cantina, each looking for something to drink.

"Still planning on helping us out up in Alaska? asked Tom.

"Well, yeah, I'd planned on heading up there in a couple of days," answered Bill.

"What's the schedule of events for you Bill?" asked Sam.

"Well, it's very close, but I have a chance at the Championship today.

"They should be announcing the winner shortly. If I win, there's a trophy and a sizable check to go with it plus a chance to move on to the Nationals one more time," answered Bill.

"As a matter of fact, I need to get out there on the fence with the other riders shortly," he continued.

"OK, let's head out there," answered Tom.

They all headed quickly back to the fence.

The speakers came alive... "Ladies and Gentlemen, the Champion of the Tucson Rodeo Bull Riding Competition and for the eighth time, a qualifier for the National Finals Rodeo... It's unanimous... Captain Wild Bill Kauffman!"

The crowd roared - "Wild Bill...!!! Wild Bill...!!!" and as they continued to chant his name, Bill leaped off the fence into the arena and took a bow, waving his hat.

He then headed to the announcers stand.

Bob stated, "I can't believe that guy!"

They all slowly and carefully climbed down off the fence.

After some time, he came back to the guys with a trophy in one hand and an envelope in the other along with an entourage of ladies gathered around him.

As he approached, he turned, waved and departed from his enthusiastic followers in a hurriedly but courteous manner.

Bill and his long lost comrades continued to walk toward the rapidly emptying parking lot.

"Captain Tom, tell me again why I need to go up to Alaska, Bill asked."

"Well Bill, no one knows the people and the outback of Alaska like you do. You've flown just about every kind of airplane there is up there and..."

"Well, this seems to be a serious project... Pay's good... Chance to do some flying in Alaska again, plus a new Cessna 206 for each of us at the end of the mission. All we have to do is deliver some mail and groceries just like the good old days. Keep our vigilance. We don't even know what we're looking for. We see something unusual, we simply report it."

Buck broke in, "Bill, I know we didn't get along real well in the old days, but I know you're one of the best there is. Working up in Bethel, I hear your name come up a lot. We need your help. Lots of hurting folks up there right now and I believe our team can dig out the problem."

"Yeah, I know Buck, I always thought you were George's favorite 'cause he assigned you the best flights pretty much on a regular basis... 20 years ago... doesn't much matter... Just don't call me 'Red'," concluded Bill.

"How'd you guys get here anyway?" he asked.

"We've got a Lear 36A sitting at the airport with engines running. With current winds, we can be in Anchorage in about four and a half hours," answered Tom.

"Tell you what.... I'll meet you at the airport in two hours. Gotta' go by home, get a shower, pick up some things, and oh yeah, continue to discuss this with my wife."

"Sounds good. How is Cindy these days," asked Tom.

"Real good... Sure has kept me happy through the years and on a good track," answered Bill."

"Glad to hear it. She's always seemed to be a nice lady. See you in a couple," concluded Tom.

"C'mon boys let's get something to eat," called Tom as he gestured toward their waiting SUV's.

Bill went by home where his wife awaited news of the Rodeo Contest. She'd gotten to the point of not watching her insane husband out there competing with guys half his age.

She was not very happy about the prospect of his taking a couple of weeks in Alaska, especially with his comrades and not her. Cindy had always worked beside her man and had spent several years there living in the Alaska bush.

She did agree however to deposit the $48,000.00 check the next day and do some preliminary shopping for their new boat - "just this time."

After a little more discussion and assurances, Bill stepped into the bedroom to pack.

"Would you drive me to the airport," he called as he continued to throw things together for his trip.

"Of course I will... Just going to miss you!" she stated.

As he came out of the bedroom with his duffle bag, he turned into the den and opened the large an-war door which revealed years of Rodeo trophies mixed with aviation memorabilia.

He stood there peering inside, "Hey... I'm goin' flying!"

He moved over some other trophies to clear a spot, then Cindy, following his moves, carefully handed him his new one.

Almost ceremoniously, he reached deeply into his front jeans pocket, pulled out a large gold belt buckle and held it up for her to see. He then removed his old buckle from his belt and replaced it with the new one.

He reached to a lower shelf and pulled out an obviously heavy medium size box, sat it on the floor, opened the top and laid his removed buckle inside atop a hundred others.

"Goin' flying in Alaska!" he reiterated and shook his head.

"Well, let's go!" exclaimed Cindy.

They rushed to the airport - Said their goodbye at the gate. Bill typed in the combination, pushed the gate open and with duffle bag over his shoulder, headed to the aircraft.

As the right engine was starting up, Tom stepped out the door and stood as if a crewmember. Just before he reached Tom and the door of the waiting Lear Jet, Bill turned to catch a last glimpse of her. Cindy, as always, waved with a great and enthusiastic smile.

As the door closed on the jet, she slowly got behind the wheel of her car and as the aircraft taxied out, somberly drove down to the end of the runway.

She pulled into the small parking area, stopped and watched for her man's departure.

After the Lear went by in the blinding fast fashion of Lear jets, she laid her head on the steering wheel, prayed that her man would come back to her, then started the car and drove away.

Likewise, Bill, broke with conversation, glanced out the window in a silent good-by to his wonderful wife of 37 years.

The aircraft climbed at 4,000 feet per minute and was out of sight within seconds.

On the climb-out, the guys again greeted each other and fell into light conversation.

The flight back was uneventful with some discussion about the mission to come, but mostly small talk about airplanes and Alaska.

'Can you top this' seemed to be the theme up until Captain Bob told his story about his Super Cub landing in deep snow story. It was the time one of his skis broke, tumbled his airplane, which literally disappeared into the powdery white landscape.

As the aircraft came to a stop, he looked around and saw all the windows were grayed out with snow, but he felt very lucky to realize he wasn't injured at all ... until... he unlocked his seatbelt. Thereafter he fell directly on his head.

Most thought the action was pretty dumb I'm sure and were contemplating what to say. However, when he said "that was pretty dumb I guess. I should have known better when I saw my peanut butter - jelly sandwich on the ceiling and I unbelted anyway - "almost killed myself!"

All laughed hysterically, including the jet pilots.

After that, the passengers quieted down, most began to drift off with their own thoughts of Alaska flying.

Chapter 13

BACK TO BUSINESS

The flight back to Anchorage went into the evening but was smooth and uneventful. After landing, they climbed into their SUV's and headed to the hotel for a good night's sleep.

The next morning early, the group had breakfast together at the hotel and proceeded back to the airport to move ahead with their somewhat mysterious assignment.

At 0800, they were sitting in the briefing room with the Colonel going over the recon mission coming up.

After the general briefing, they climbed aboard the Lear again and left for Avionics and Simulator Training in Galena.

All had a somewhat tough time learning the new technology however, all had mastered it to a good degree.

They were just completing their third day of training, when the instructor received a phone call.

As he hung up the phone, "Gentlemen, your Avionics and Simulator training are complete. I know we had another day to wind things up, but the Colonel wants you back in Anchorage right away."

"I believe all of you have a good handle on your avionics and equipment, however, any specific questions before dismissal?"

"No... We're good. Fine with me..." stated several different guys.

"Good," he continued, "The Lear should be here in about an hour. Pick up your gear and head out to the terminal... Hangar Five... Good Luck."

"Thanks," stated several guys.

As they were leaving the building to get their gear, Bill, Jerry and Bob caught up with Tom, "Tom, we were planning on really paying attention the next couple of days on this G3000 system, but now school's out."

"Can you give us a quick course when we get down to Anchorage?"

The group continued walking.

"No problem, I'll give it to you right now. Ready?"

They broke out their notebooks as they continued their fast walking pace.

"OK. Here goes," Tom continued. "Type in where ever you want to go. Then hit the D button for Direct to. Press Enter twice and go there."

"Sound simple enough?" he asked.

"Now that does sound pretty darn simple," answered Bob.

Tom continued, "The rest you can work out through osmosis, then if all else fails and you're tired of pushing buttons, pull out the book and read the directions."

"Sounds good. Thanks for that thorough briefing," as they all laughed at their practical joke.

Tom smirked and shook his head.

Jerry looked at the chuckling men, "I wasn't kidding you guys!"

Tom turned, "I've got a mock up panel already aboard. We can review any functions you'd like to on the way to Anchorage."

"Alright," Jerry said with a smile.

The flight down was uneventful and educational for some. They all took glances downward from 35,000 feet looking for any unusual patterns.

After arriving back in Anchorage, the men grabbed their gear from the baggage compartment and proceeded through already open doors into the building. Shortly, they arrived at the Colonel's office.

Tom tapped the door three times.

"Enter," was heard through the door.

As they began to enter the office, Colonel Bill pointed toward the boardroom table.

After all were seated at the table, he began, "I am sorry for breaking you off from your training, but we feel we have to get you out into the field as soon as possible."

"Two incidents - another blocked runway at Kalskag up on the Kuskokwim River, and two missing persons from the Kaley mine southeast of Bethel."

"The Troopers are on it but nothing's coming up."

"There's a possibility, that whoever's closing down these runways are simply buying time to make a move or to move something around unseen."

The Colonel gestured at an area on the map of the peninsula north of Bethel and continued, "And, if they have a group of folks that could block all the decent runways at once in a coordinated manner, they could effectively cut off this entire Bethel peninsula for several days."

"However, I know of seven Cessna 206 aircraft that can land practically anywhere, with seven of the best and most experienced bush pilots running them. Those pilots could be in Bethel in a couple of days to begin making their passenger and freight runs."

"What do you say Gentlemen?" the Colonel asked.

Tom glanced at each individual to get a yes or no. All responded affirmatively with a small head nod.

"We're ready sir," answered Tom for the men.

"Very well, here's our tentative plan," the Colonel continued, "Once on the job so to speak, you're free to move about in any fashion, but with the total facade of delivering cargo and supplies. Your schedule will be roughly set by Mr. Tim Vestal at West Alaska Air in Bethel where you'll be assigned a daily run with multiple stops."

"What about flight training... Some of us haven't been in a 206 in years," asked Wild Bill.

"Well, you will be on your own for a couple of days, and since you're all flight instructors, you can team up for training and get in some actual aircraft experience," answered the Colonel.

"I recommend you work outside of the Anchorage Bowl area and utilize remote strips for your takeoffs and landings. For your overnights, plan to rough it in tents when possible so as not to attract attention."

"The bottom line is that we need all of you in Bethel by Thursday morning."

He noticed the guys glancing at each other, "Seems tough I know, but as Tom has mentioned to you guys, if your mission is successful and we find and capture some bad guys, remember, the 206's are yours."

"We'll get you whatever paint job you want... whatever interior you want. You can keep the trick avionics package as well."

"Now that's very impressive!" concluded Tom as the guys again glanced at each other.

"Remember. You are eyes and ears for us! Recon only... Good luck Gentlemen," the Colonel concluded.

All the men stood, came forward and shook hands with the Colonel.

As they proceeded out the door and into the large hangar, Sam tugged on Toms arm and leaned toward him, "Eyes and Ears?"

"What do we need all that firepower for...? ... Bullet proof windows?"

"I'm sure that's all just precautionary," Tom whispered. "They just want us civilians to be totally safe out there."

The next day, the aircraft left singly, staggered every half hour, so as to blend in with other departing traffic.

The men, worked with and played with their aircraft, getting used to handling characteristics and worked with the new avionics. Tom was the last one out of Anchorage.

Shortly after leaving Anchorage approach, he glanced at his VFR chart to ensure he would enter the correct pass to cross the Alaska Range.

"Tom, you up yet?" called Sam on a discreet radio frequency.

"I'm up," answered Tom.

"The guys were asking and all are waiting at our designated coordinates as you asked. Be advised, there's a ceiling in the pass, roughly 3,000 feet. I'm about 10 minutes out," stated Sam.

"Thanks Sam. Be there shortly, about 15," stated Tom.

"Test this JATO System Power out before the pass," he mumbled to himself.

"Ok..," as he eased the throttle forward. "150 knots... 160... 170... 180... 190... 200... 210... 220... 230... 240... 250... 260... OK..." as he throttled back.

"Still four minutes to go... That's fast enough for a Cessna 206!" he exclaimed as he approached the pass entrance.

Again, he enjoyed the proximity of nature's best scenery on both sides of his aircraft as he moved carefully through the snow covered rock walled airway.

The flight through was smooth sailing for Tom and his men who'd all been through there a hundred times.

As Tom came out of Rainy Pass, he had purposefully descended to a very low altitude and had to bank quickly right then left to pass between large monolith rocks.

"Just checking... You never know when you've got to get low, very low," he mumbled again.

Following another large natural wash area of the mountainside, the normally abandoned airstrip came into view.

As he set up for his final approach, he glanced back and upward at the spectacular 8,000 foot snow covered mountains he'd just exited.

"I can't believe I'm still getting paid to do this," he mumbled to himself. Don't believe anyone will find us here," he continued and thought,

'What a magnificent setting for the beginning of their clandestine and possibly perilous adventure!'

Chapter 14

FAREWELL, ALASKA AND THE BEAR

As he approached the old airstrip, he thought to himself... 'Farewell, Alaska, population one, he hoped, and also hoped that his good friend 'Jed' Williams would be there. With the increase in solar flares, talking on Jed's obsolete government radio / telephone was practically impossible resulting in at times little or no communication with the outside world.'

Sam reported on their discreet frequency, "Tom... Might want to stay to the right of center a little... Watch for the rocks scattered along the runway and on both sides."

"Thanks Sam," answered Tom as he selected full flaps.

He touched down and rolled out avoiding most of the rocks but caught a couple of good bumps.

He carefully taxied over to line up with the rest of the aircraft.

After shut down, he glanced down the line and noticed all were covering their aircraft with the white camouflage covers given to them by the Colonel.

Sam approached, "Tom, I think you missed a couple of those boulders. You might want to give it another try and see if you can actually hit every one of them!"

Tom laughed as Jerry and Sam began helping him secure his aircraft.

After all was settled on the ramp, they proceeded on and entered a large abandoned hangar.

"Think they'll find us?" asked Sam. "I know Mother will be about soon looking around... testing her equipment."

"Everybody have their GPS tracking devices?" asked Tom loudly.

"Sure do," some answered as they all dug into their pockets.

Tom pulled out a bag but instead of taking them, gave each pilot the small credit card protectors.

Slip your 'GTD' in one of these and keep them handy for when they're needed.

As Tom placed his tracking chip in his small lead based 'protector', "Just wanted to make a point to the Colonel, that we're somewhat capable of taking care of ourselves."

"Men... In the early morning, let's plan on a couple of hours practice. Everybody get honed up on your maneuvers, especially your takeoffs and landings. It would be wise to use the JATO system power at least once before we get to Bethel," he concluded.

They all agreed.

"Anyone around at all?" Tom questioned the men.

"You mean someone actually lives here?" questioned an amused Jimmy.

"There used to be a caretaker that lived here full time," answered Tom.

"Let's break out something to eat... get some rest. We've got a big day tomorrow," he called to the men.

The men began breaking out their M R E's and looking for a place to bed down.

Suddenly, a heavy knock on the steel door.

The guys pulled weapons and eased to the sides of the room.

Tom opened the door.

Standing there was a large burly, bearded man, in overalls over an army green sweat shirt.

"Jediah! Hoped I'd run across you out here," greeted Tom enthusiastically as he stepped forward and reached for a hand shake.

Jed stepped forward grabbed Toms hand and pulled him into a manly hug with a slap on the back.

"Why, Captain Tom, long time no see. Heck, long time no see anyone. What's all this?" he asked.

"Well, we're delivering those 206 aircraft to West Alaska Air up in Bethel to use on some of their routes."

"We're flying for them for a while just to get their guys trained... just thought we'd stop in here for a visit."

"Sounds good," as he glanced knowingly at the automatic shotguns being placed back against the wall and noticed all the pilots had Glock pistols on their sides.

"Must be gettin' more dangerous to fly groceries these days," he said with a light chuckle as he glanced around the room.

"Good to see you Captain Tom," he continued. "Make yourselves at home."

He turned as if to leave, "Say, if you guys are really practicing maneuvers around here tomorrow, would you keep an eye out for a real fat Griz with half a cow in his kitchen?"

"He took it two days ago and I'm sure he's still eating on it. I took a shot at the bear... may have hit it. Sure would like to finish it off before he gets my other one."

"Two questions Jed," asked Tom, "How in the world did you get two cows here... and two... how did you know we would be out practicing maneuvers tomorrow?" asked Tom.

"Well, a friend at Northern Air was taking the cows to a homesteader strip out near Bethel last year and the runway was blocked off. They landed over in Bethel but couldn't make contact with the folks," answered Jed.

"Did anyone ever find out what happened there?" Tom asked.

"Not really. The troopers took a helicopter out there from Bethel and found no sign of the young couple... Seemed to just vanish... Figured they were out hunting and got hunted by some varmint."

Jed continued, "Well Northern Air was headed back to Fairbanks, had engine trouble and landed here."

"I just took care of the guys, kept 'em fed and warm for a couple of nights while they were working on the plane. After the repairs, they still didn't feel that comfortable about the engine, needed to go out as light as possible, left the rest of the cargo, including the cows."

"I've had plenty of milk, butter and even learned how to make cheese."

"That dang bar' tore the front of my barn off the other day, tore the head off my best cow and took off with the carcass."

"By the time I got my gun, he was just about out of range. I took a shot anyway, thought I saw him jerk, but it was twilight and couldn't say for sure."

"I'm thinking if I don't kill him, he'll continue to feed around here. I know they don't like the taste of human beans but they seem to enjoy shredding up people."

"I'd go after him myself, but after all I am the Mayor now," as he pointed to a plaque on the wall over an old military desk... "and, I need to stay pretty close to town," he concluded.

As the guys looked at each other questioningly, Jed raised both arms in victory, "It was a landslide election with no recount needed."

"I elected myself," Jed again concluded.

"Sure Mr. Mayor," as Tom glanced at some of the guys... "We'll locate him for you," answered Tom.

"Thanks Tom," as he nodded and smiled.

As he gave a sweeping gesture to the men, "You guys make yourself at home for the night. I've already kicked the heat on.

He turned to leave, "I'll see about drumming up some breakfast for you guys in the morning."

"Oh, Jediah," What about how you knew we were training in the morning?" Tom asked as he grabbed Jed's elbow.

"Well, actually I heard you," he answered.

"When this place was in its hey-day about 35 years ago, they had a listening device network in place, not sure what for, but every building has several microphones all networked to the office. I just found it when doing my barn repairs, traced the wiring and found a hidden room down below the office, like a command center bunker. Plugged it all back in and it works fine as long as my generator's working... Seemed a convenient way to keep an eye on things. Now that I know who you are, I'll shut off this building."

"Thanks Jed. Could I see the bunker sometime?" Tom asked.

"Sure, come on over right now if you'd like," Jed replied.

Tom grabbed his coat as they proceeded out the door into the darkening, chilly Alaska evening.

"So Jeff... I mean Jed, I can't believe you're still out here!" commented Tom as they left out of hearing range of the men.

"Oh, I get out from time to time," he answered.

He pointed to a somewhat in descript building where they continued toward.

As they entered the unlocked office, "Like some coffee...Just made it an hour ago," he asked.

"Sure," answered Tom.

Jeff pulled another cup from the overhead cabinet and poured the coffee, then turned to sit the pot back on the small stove.

"Long time since Gia Le," mentioned Tom.

"Yep... Long time," answered Jeff still with his back to him.

Tom noticed Jeff was peering out the window deep in thought.

'Jefferson Davis Smith, alias Jediah, after his service years seemed to love disguises and fooling everyone. I was sure he was here working for the CIA, NSA, or undercover for some other agency.'

'Some combat vets took things harder than others and after Vietnam; we didn't even know what PTSD was much less how to deal with it.'

'His case was a hard one. He was based at Gia Le with a long time growing up friend Adam Larson. Adam, a blue eyed sandy haired kid from Nebraska had turned 21 about a week before. We'd celebrated his birthday by grilling a bartered for steak over a grill we'd made from a drum cut in half.

He was always kidding around and seemed to bring light into a room with his humor and positive attitude.

The evening before we were scheduled out, Adam had received a 'Dear John' letter from his wife of one year asking for a divorce. He was taking it pretty hard knowing he had less than 30 days left on the tour and would be out of the service within two months.

Jeff spent several hours attempting to console Adam but finally gave up and crashed out about midnight.

The next day, our mission was simply a short security recon not even a mile outside our perimeter.

As we departed for the recon, Adam jokingly commented, "Wouldn't it be funny if I stepped on a landmine today." He laughed. "That should wind things up nicely for my short wonderful life."

Jeff shook his head, "Adam, you shouldn't say things like that. The Spoken Word you know. Besides, one of us might get hit as well."

"Yeah, OK, sorry," he answered.

About an hour into our recon, Adam stepped on some sort of mine, a small shaped charge of some sort; it literally blew him into pieces 20 feet from Jeff.

All of us were knocked down by the blast, but not one of us was hit with shrapnel.

The event was very hard on all of us, especially for Jeff who became a basket case for a several weeks. Eventually, he was sent home.

Although, Adam was his best friend, Jeff had not been able to handle the task of clearing Adams locker, so I took care of it, gathered and packed his things, including pictures of his young wife and family. I then took it upon myself to send it all to his Mom and Dad's address.

Other than the horror of seeing that happen and experiencing the great loss, we could not help but feel that it could have been any one of us going home in that sealed casket.'

Jeff turned away from the window and back toward Tom, "I'm just glad to see you Tom."

"Likewise Jeff..." Tom answered.

That small statement seemed to somewhat console their kindred spirits.

Tom moved on, "Are you following the situation up in the northwest?"

"Somewhat... Whatever's going on is so subtle and well cloaked that our satellites can't pick up anything unusual," Jeff spoke in a normal tone.

"I understand that all the forces are ready to get out there, but holding for something to break. Guess that's where you boys come in huh?" Jeff stated and asked.

"Guess so," answered Tom.

As they finished their coffee, Jeff turned to the left and slid a small roll top desk to the side which exposed a half size door.

"Got to practically crawl to get in here," he laughed as he stooped and led the way.

As he entered, he flipped on the lights.

"Come on in... Room for about four or five folks in here," Jeff stated.

"Wow! This is something. You say this is at least 35 years old?" Tom asked.

"Well, I've added a few things. Once in a while, our communication guys come out and modify this or that," answered Jeff.

"They know we're here don't they," asked Tom.

"Not really, I did get a call about two hours ago. The Colonel was inquiring. Hadn't seen you at that time - told him I'd let him know if you stopped by."

"Thanks for not calling," stated Tom.

As Tom continued to scrutinize the electronic panels, "This section has some unusual devices. I understand what an oscilloscope is as well as a magnetometer and a seismic table meter, but what's this system - E M Monitoring Solutions, and this, Ano... Ano...ma-listic Target Acquisition, Gravimeter, Magnetic Variometer? What is all this?"

"I could tell you Tom, but then I'd have to kill you," Jeff chuckled.

"Tell you the truth, I have no idea what that old junk is," he concluded.

"Must have been more going on here back in the seventies," stated Tom.

"Anyway, not sure what all that has to do with the Cold War or any listening post. Maybe they were protecting us from Aliens," Tom said sarcastically.

"You could be right," Jeff said without sarcasm.

"You're a good friend Jeff," stated Tom.

Tom continued, "We're going to find out what's going on up there, but first, we will find your bear before we leave.

"Sounds good. Would you like something to drink?" asked Jeff.

"No thanks. Should get back to the guys... get a plan together," Tom answered.

With overcast skies, night had fallen quickly. All appreciated sleeping inside rather than in their tents.

At first light, Bob and Wild Bill followed the Grizzly's tracks part way up the hill side to get his direction. Looking with Binoculars they could not see any sign of the bear.

"Let's take off and see if we can locate the bear," suggested Bill.

"Good idea," answered Bob. They both glanced at Tom. Tom waved them on.

They turned and walked toward the aircraft.

"Jed, I'm sure you'll get a good handle on where the bear might be in a few minutes," said Tom.

The two aircraft took off, both demonstrating short field technique to begin their practice. Shortly they disappeared over the small hills staying low level.

Shortly, they heard one of the aircraft engines racing as if in a dive. Everyone ran to get into position to see the action.

As the first aircraft came into view, they realized he was diving toward the ground with landing lights on. At low level, he pulled up in an oblique turn to the right.

Next the other 206 appeared in the same position with engine racing, then pulled up abruptly in an oblique turn to the left.

"What are those guys doing?" questioned Sam as he picked up the portable radio.

"Gentlemen... W<u>hat</u> are you doing?"

"Found him Capt'n," answered Wild Bill... "Herding him down toward town... You might want to let the Mayor know."

"You know, according to State Regulations, we can't fly and shoot the same day... but he could - in self-defense of his town."

Wild Bill and Bear Man Bob continued taking turns running down at the bear and chasing him toward the outskirts of town.

After several passes, "This is Bear Man... Should be coming around a small building just to the south of the old FAA building in about three minutes."

The mayor ran inside his cabin office and came out with his 12 gauge double barrel shotgun.

"Thanks Bob, the Mayor's got his 12 gauge and is coming around the west side of the City Hall building," called Tom.

"One more push should move him in range," called Wild Bill as he zoomed down to the other side of one of the outbuildings and pulled up with his wheel knocking off snow along with some roof shingles.

The bear, now totally enraged came tearing around the corner toward City Hall. Jed, in his anxiousness to get into a better position, tripped on a loose board, fell to his knee and discharged one of his barrels. The bear turned immediately toward the kneeling Jed.

He took aim quickly and let go the other barrel which knocked the bear down. The bear rolled once, but quickly staggered to his feet again and charged.

"Lookout!" Sam called as he jumped into the open from around another small building. Tom stepped up behind Jed with his shotgun ready hoping Jed would get reloaded and kill the bear himself.

At the last possible moment, all the guys stepped out and opened up with their Glocks at close range, practically tearing the bears left front leg off.

Obviously all were shooting at the left front quarter to break the bear down.

As the bear slid to a stop just short of the Mayor, covering him with dust and debris, he sat back on the ground, "How about that boys. Now, I've got a three legged bear rug and plenty of meat for the winter! Plus, I'm not dead!"

"Thanks Guys!" called a thankful Jediah.

"Let's help Jed skin out this bear and have some bear steaks for breakfast!" said Tom.

"I'll do the cookin'," said Jed as he climbed onto his feet.

The two aircraft landed, and as the guys approached, Sam asked, "That enough training for you guys?"

"Sure is," answered all the pilots practically in unison.

"You guys were not even in the air," as he gestured to Mike, Jimmy and Jerry.

"Yeah, we know Tom. But just watching that rodeo was plenty for today," answered Jimmy.

"Ok. Let's get him skinned out, eat a steak and get on the road," agreed Tom.

"After breakfast, I'll give the Colonel a call; let him know where we are. Then we probably better head on out to Bethel... get started on our program," he concluded.

Chapter 15

PLANS CHANGE

After breakfast, as Tom prepared to call the Colonel, his satellite phone rang.

"We've got a problem Tom," said the Colonel in a matter of fact voice.

"Mother was about to leave shortly behind you yesterday but regretfully, she's been sabotaged."

"In what way Colonel?" asked Tom

"They were taxiing out when both engines began to overheat. The guys shut down and were towed back," the Colonel answered.

"What we found early this morning is that the over-heat was caused by some sort of caustic sand like material in the oil. Looks like both engines will have to be torn down. We have one extra engine, but have to find another one."

"Any suspects?" asked Tom.

"Not sure but with our security, it has to be someone on the inside," continued the Colonel.

"We do have one in custody at the moment. He's a new mechanic, a fellow up from the lower forty eight, came with good credentials but he was the only one caught on camera around the aircraft last evening."

"Looked like on the camera that he put normal oil in, which he claims he did, but we're holding him until we get some answers."

"That doesn't sound good Colonel," commented Tom.

"You're right Tom... Doesn't look good. They may have you in their sites as well with the GPS Tracking devices we installed."

"Ok, we'll take care of the tracking devices," stated Tom.

"This is probably a deeper and a more sophisticated problem than we anticipated. We haven't been able to get anything out of this guy... yet."

"Sounds like we're pretty much on our own out here Colonel," continued Tom. "Better not even go into Bethel, especially as a group. I'm thinking we should split up and just take a good look around. We'll find something. We're at home out here."

"Where are you now? We lost tracking when you entered the Alaskan Range," asked the Colonel.

"Like to tell you sir but probably shouldn't discuss much on the phone, especially if they're inside the company," answered Tom.

"No problem. There's a secondary discrete number inside the case of your phone. I've left it there in case something happened such as a spy among us. I'll activate it now on your satellite phone with a backup number for another person in case something were to happen to me. You know, down with the flu, flat tire on the way to work or something," in the jest of trading back some of Tom's humor.

"Thanks Colonel," Tom responded. "I'll get that number and give you a call with our tentative plan."

He hung up the phone and began removing the cover.

Sam, had listened to the conversation just ended, "Why don't I make a quick call to Will. Get him to plow the runway at the ranch. We can get organized, pick up a few supplies and have a good sendoff meal. I've also got two 300 gallon tanks of Avgas I forgot to mention the other day. We can top off as well."

"Good idea Sam. That would put us in a good strategic position to work from. We could use your ranch as our rendezvous point for some of the time as well. Plus, a good sendoff meal is not a bad idea either."

"Probably should make the call from Jed's bush phone. I'm sure he won't mind."

"I'll get him right away," said Sam as he threw his jacket on and headed toward the door."

"And let Will know we really appreciate his help and after that call, would you get the guys in here for a briefing?"

"Will do."

"Thanks."

Tom sat down at the old metal military desk, pulled his charts and notebook from his flight bag and began to prepare his briefing notes.

As the guys filtered back inside, Sam confirmed, "Just talked to Will. He'll have the runway plowed within one hour."

"Thanks Sam," said Tom as he made note of the time on his watch.

As the guys gathered inside the building, "Gentlemen, our mission guidelines have changed. Same mission, but we've lost our backup support that included surveillance and firepower. Mother's been sabotaged and will not be available for a few days."

"'Could be a little more hazardous than first indicated and if anyone would like to call it quits, I totally understand," began Tom.

All looked around at each other.

Jerry, "Are you kidding, I'm having the time of my life Captain!"

"We all are," the guys said in unison.

"Okay then."

"Plans are to stop in and regroup at Sam's Ranch over near Lime Village."

"Quick question" interrupted Jimmy, "Why not just go on over to Bethel and get started on our routes from there?"

"Jim, in speaking with the Colonel, the company has reason to believe that our mission possibly has been compromised and that someone may be expecting us there and not in a good way," Tom answered.

"I understand," stated Jim.

Tom turned back to the group, "First off, we'll let Sam lead the way as he knows the route better than anyone."

Your sequence for departure is Sam - 'Sampson', Jimmy - 'Jimbo', Bob - 'Bear Man', Bill - 'Wild Bill', Jerry - 'Bag Man', Michael - 'Buck' and myself - 'Iceman'. On the way over, plan to keep about two miles separation."

"Weather is good, but in case you lose sight of your lead aircraft, the ranch sits along the Stony River on the Sparravohn 014 degree radial four miles upriver from Lime Village."

"As he turned and pointed at the chart, "I'd like for you to all fly south, low and close to the mountains, use whatever terrain you can to conceal your flight. It's a follow the leader operation and not a competition. Use the ravines and so on, just don't hit any hills."

"When you get to the river, turn right and stay low at or below the banks if you can till you see the ranch and airstrip. There's not going to be any markings, smoke or other indication of the landing strip from above. Your instrument guidelines are that at four point three miles from Lime Village airport, 2AK you should be at 300 feet, at approach speed, full flaps and parallel to and just to the right of the river bank. Your landing direction is two seven zero degrees."

"Use short field technique as you only have 750 feet of runway. At four point zero miles, you're there."

"Sam's son, Will is continuing to clear a nice parking area for all our aircraft off to the right of the Runway. He'll direct you to your spot with the snow machine. Cover your aircraft quickly."

"He can trailer the fuel tank and will top us off while we get some grub. From there, we'll fine tune our plans for the recon mission."

"Think about what area you would prefer to recon and we'll discuss and assign areas to each aircraft."

"Any questions? All good?" asked Tom.

"We're good... Let's do it!" shouted Jimmy.

There were no other questions and the guys began gearing up to depart Farewell.

Tom walked quickly over to Jediah's office to say thanks for the meals and accommodations.

"Hey Jediah," spoke Tom as he stepped slightly inside the office.

"Heading out?" asked Jed.

"Heading out," replied Tom, "Appreciate the meals and accommodations."

"My pleasure sir," replied Jed. . Thank you for the fine bear steaks in my freezer.

No problem," replied Tom.

After a thoughtful moment, Tom continued, "Say Jed, I might check back in with you when this mission's over. Sure would like to know more about some of the history around here."

"Sounds great Tom. We'll keep a light on for you!"

"Thanks... Ok. Who's <u>we</u>?" questioned Tom.

"Oh, you know - Betsy and me," answered Jed as he gazed out the window for a moment.

He turned back toward Tom, grinned, "What the heck... See you a little later Captain." They shook hands with a military hug and slap on the back.

"Comrade!" said Tom, then turned, stepped out the door and departed at a fast clip.

"Good Flight," yelled Jed at the door.

Tom waved his arm while walking and looking straight ahead.

Tom remembered some of the times they'd had in the old days in and out of Gia Le. 'Guess he never got over some of those ugly events he'd encountered as a 'LRRP' and then to have your best friend blown to bits right in front of you...'

He chose not to let his thoughts go any further and began to jog toward his small fleet.

'I'll be back.'

CHAPTER 16

LUNCH AT SAM'S PLACE

After a follow the leader squadron flight through some spectacular scenery, they were all now down low following the Stony River on a straight in approach to Sam's air strip.

They landed on the short snow covered strip, then taxied in single file to the parking area Will had just finished clearing.

Will sat on his tractor off to the side and watched as the pilots shut down their engines.

The men hurriedly got out, performed a post flight inspection and secured their white parachute type covers over each aircraft.

All waited beside their practically invisible planes until Tom had landed and parked, then several helped cover his aircraft as well.

"Let's head up to the house men... Get that grill going Will!" ordered Sam.

As they approached the cabin, Sam called to the men, "Just head inside, we can eat in the great room."

They pulled up some extra chairs and all fit around Sam's table.

After a great steak and potatoes type lunch, Tom walked up to the large wall map. Sam followed.

Tom began, "Just keep your seats gentlemen. We can get started on our briefing right here."

"I suggest we begin our recon here and... here, pointing to villages on the Yukon as well as the lower Kusko Rivers within 150 miles of the coast."

"I agree," stated Sam. "From the reports we've heard, most of the incidents and disappearances are within that arc."

Tom continued, "I spoke with Colonel Bill on the way here. He mentioned there had been another incident up at Wales last night. An aircraft was sabotaged and hazardous debris had been thrown over the runway."

"My thoughts are that these incidents as he points to the map are possibly diversionary tactics. Something could be going on somewhere south of the Yukon where not too much has been reported."

"Diversionary, now that sounds plumb military Captain Tom... Shouldn't we let the military get more involved at this point?" asked Jimmy.

"Not yet. They have no idea who or what they're dealing with," as he headed back to the table.

Will stepped into the room, "All the planes are fueled and ready."

"Thanks Will," stated Tom..."Great meal too. We really appreciate it."

All the guys agreed with a general, "Thanks Will."

"Drag up a chair. You can sit in on the rest of the brief," stated Tom.

As Will eased his chair into the corner of the room, Tom continued, "Gentlemen, both Sam's and my gut feeling is that this is not any kind of a civilian matter, however, we're not ruling out smugglers working on a grand scale but somehow remaining invisible to the authorities."

He continued his briefing to his very alert team, "It seems logical that it's connected to the coast somehow as all occurrences are within a hundred miles or so of the Bethel peninsula."

"To begin our recon, I would like for you to team up by two's and remain within radio range of each other in case of a mechanical or any other reason where you would need some assistance."

"From these three points, as he points to three different points on the map, we can work our way over to the coast and ease on into the Bethel area."

"Bob and Bill, I would like for you to proceed west south west and pick up anything in between, such as the Taylor Mountain area and work the area south of V319 but stay north of the Togiak River area."

"You can overnight wherever you prefer, but just check in and let me know where."

"Sam and Jimmy, you've got a long run out to Holy Cross, Russian Mission, Anvik, Grayling, Shagaluk and the Innoko River Basin. Probably best to overnight at Holy Cross but if something different, let me know. The next day work your way on down river toward Bethel."

"Jerry, you're with me back up to the McGrath area. We'll work along the Kusko and go as far north as Nikolai, then back down river by way of Crooked Creek and Sleepmute areas and overnight at Red Devil."

"The next day we'll continue down toward Aniak and Kalskag and work on toward Bethel."

"Mike, if ok with you, I'll give you a long run directly toward Bethel, but search out any areas of interest along your route. After arrival in the Bethel area, I would like for you to continue to work in and around the area since you've recently been working down there."

"All of you try to interact somewhat with the locals. Perhaps you can pick up something."

"You should always be able to get one of the teams on the radio, but if not you can use your satellite phone to get me."

"Sound ok?" he asked.

"You bet Tom. I'm rearing to go," answered Mike.

"All you guys, keep an eye out for any airstrips or anything that looks like an airstrip, or even new roads. Watch for any unusual structures or any type of construction equipment just seemingly sitting around."

"Work out your own grids between you as you go. Keep good notes of your routing, as a matter of fact, its low tech, but use yellow highlighter to mark your flight routes covered. That will give us something to go on later to see if there's any areas we've missed."

"Men, here's the new number for the Colonel," as he wrote it on his board. Use it if you have no contact with first myself, then Sam. Any team member can relay messages as well to us."

"Weapons... Sam?" asked Tom.

"Anything you want and feel comfortable with." answered Sam.

Tom continued, "Load up whatever weapons you feel you might need in case we run into a problem. Use the cargo tubes for your longer weapons and as needed."

"Any questions?" Tom asked of the group.

With silence indicating no questions, the meeting broke up with the guys clearing the table and placing their dishes in the sink.

They headed out onto the porch and followed Sam over to the armory. They went through the plethora of weaponry and carried away everything from AK 47's to grenade launchers and grenades.

"Got any 16's?" Tom asked, "My favorite weapon."

"Sure, here they are," as Sam opened another cabinet.

"Well, guys," Tom continued, "just remember... We're Recon only and defensive only. If you see anything get on the horn and move away."

"Any questions and all agreed?" Tom asked with closure.

"All agreed... Hoo-ra-a-ah," in unison as they headed out with arms and ammunition toward their waiting aircraft.

CHAPTER 17

RECON- THE SEARCH BEGINS

The rest of the day, all searched and landed at every conceivable airstrip possible and spoke with the locals when possible.

All had meticulously searched for any clues, abnormality or any indication of a problem.

There was no sign of anything as they all continued to work toward Bethel.

By the end of the day, Sam and Jimmy had spent a lot of energy and had run low on fuel and decided to head on over to Holy Cross where Sam looked up an old friend. They both spent the night as a guest at his house.

Tom and Jerry finished up and also running low on fuel, headed to Red Devil. Tom called ahead and spoke with the manager there. "Come on in, we've plenty of room and plenty of 100A," was the response received.

After landing on the well-kept gravel field, they were met by a pickup with an armed driver and a couple of guards.

After removing their gear, they secured and covered their aircraft.

"Sure don't see any buildings Tom," mentioned Jerry somewhat unsure about their night.

"Oh, you'll see. We've got everything we need," answered Tom.

After a short 10 minute drive, they arrived and entered a small tunnel that led into a good sized underground parking garage.

They saw the well-lighted main door to the facility when entering the garage and both felt somewhat relieved. After they thanked the driver and grabbed their gear, they headed toward the main door to the facility.

Upon entering, they realized they had entered an Airlock entrance and proceeded to the secondary door.

Tom held the door as Jerry entered.

"Wow! What a place," remarked Jerry as he viewed the atrium style building inside the mountain, "This is not a building, it's an underground city!"

Although Tom had been there on several occasions, he also was in awe of the open architectural design of the totally self-contained city.

They were met by the general manager, shown their rooms and were invited down to chow 'in 20 minutes'.

Both felt right at home in this alien environment and were looking forward to a good night's rest.

Meanwhile, Bob and Wild Bill had both departed from their last strips of the day.

"Bear Man, you up?" called Bill.

"Just in the air Wild Bill," answered Bob as he climbed out above the terrain.

"Think we better head up to Holy Cross for the night?" questioned Bill.

"Not hardly... I'm more in the mood for a nice chunk of Salmon or Halibut in Bethel," answered Bob.

"If that's the case, I wouldn't mind getting a nice hotel room myself, get a good shower and a good night's sleep," agreed Bill.

"You know... There's something called the Logan House that's a pretty darn good place to overnight," continued Bill.

"Captain Tom did kinda leave it up to us more or less. Didn't say we couldn't go into Bethel. We could get a good night's rest, chat with the locals, just nose around for a while," continued Bob.

"Let's go, just 25 minutes away. Did you plan it that way Bear Man?" asked Bill.

"Who me?" asked Bob.

"Oh, by the way, in the Bethel area, drop the 'Wild Bill handle'. Just call me W.B," asked Bill.

"No problem W.B," answered Bob. "Let's head on over."

They both typed in BET on their magic screens and turned directly to Bethel.

While they were on their way, Tom called them on their satellite phones...,"Wild Bill, Bear Man... This is Iceman... Are you up?"

"Wild Bill here." "Bear Man here," they answered.

"Conference call gentlemen..."

"Just got a call from Tim at West Alaska Air. Since you're the closest, he's suggested you both overnight at Bethel tonight and park in his hangar overnight."

"The reason is that there's a possibility that the closer we get to the coastal areas, we're going to need somebody capable of getting down on the water."

"They can outfit both your aircraft onto floats if that's ok with you," he inquired.

"No Problem, seems like good advice. Haven't been on floats for a while. It will feel good," answered Bill.

"Same here," answered Bob.

"Ok. Work directly with Tim to coordinate security and your getting back out tomorrow as soon as possible."

"Iceman...," Bill interjected, "In the Bethel area, just call me W.B."

"Sure can Wild Bill. We'll go with W.B. from here," answered Tom.

"Thanks Iceman. I can explain later on," concluded Bill.

"Guess you're going under cover under cover," said Bob with a grin.

They both chuckled, imagining some kind of social aspect in his early history.

Bear Man and W.B. signed off and proceeded on toward the Bethel airport.

After landing, they taxied straightaway onto the ramp and were directed to Tim's hangar. The large doors were opening and both were flagged into the hangar. The large hangar doors immediately were slammed shut.

Tim, the owner of the air service approached as they were unloading their overnight gear, "Bob, Bill - Tim Vestal here. I've got you a couple of rooms over at the Logan House. Your car's outside. We'll have your floats on, aircraft fueled and ready to pull out at 0800 hours."

"Sounds good Tim. Thanks," answered Bob as he began pulling out and reorganizing some of his gear.

"Don't worry about your aircraft or your weapons. We're quite secure here," Tim concluded as he threw the car keys to Bob.

"Thanks Tim," as they grabbed their overnight bag and headed toward the door.

As they opened the side door to leave, both glanced at each other, turned and walked back to their aircraft.

Rifling through their covered cargo areas, both came up with their shoulder holsters.

They removed their coats briefly, put on the holsters, reached under the front seat, pulled out their Glocks from their cases, checked that they were loaded, inserted the deadly weapons and pulled on their coats. Again, they headed for the door.

Several mechanics began working quickly on the first aircraft.

They attached Bob's Cessna onto their normal lift to get started on the float installation. As they increased hydraulic pressure to raise the aircraft off the floor, the lead mechanic, "This is the heaviest 206 I've ever tried to get up... How about we parallel these two winch motors to get this thing off the floor."

The second mechanic just shook his head at the fact as they continued with the unusual 206's.

After a short drive, Bob and Bill arrived in the lobby of the hotel, parked their car near the door facing outward and proceeded to check in.

"Two rooms for us?" asked Bob.

"Sure do. One of you Wild Bill?" asked the clerk.

Bill pointed to Bob, "That's him."

The clerk nodded as he looked at Bob's wavy dark hair, "Thought Wild Bill had red hair."

With a grin, he handed them their room keys, "Tim said to give Bear Man and Wild Bill good rooms for the night. I'm just a rodeo fan -   Watched that bull ride down in Tucson about a week ago."

As Bill stuffed the key into his front pocket, the clerk caught a glimpse of W.B.s National Rodeo Championship belt buckle.

"Might want to cover that up Bear Man," he smirked as he pointed to the gold and silver buckle.

"Thanks," said Bill.

As they walked out of earshot of the teller, "Why'd you say that Bill?"

Bill shrugged and smiled.

"I forgot you've got a rep out here - probably a few enemies too..." speculated Bob.

"If you'd really like to know, I worked undercover for a while here, busted some drug and alcohol dealers big time. My cover was never blown... so I believe."

"Took a knife right here," as he pulled up his shirt on the right side. "Spect' they're all out of prison about now," he concluded.

Bob shook his head, "Yeah that's dangerous business alright."

"Sure is," answered Bill.

As they approached the stairs, Bob asked, "Downstairs about 7:30?"

"You bet," answered Bill.

Both crashed into bed for a short rest, then got together for dinner at 7:30.

As they finished up a fairly quiet meal, Bob suggested," If you're about through with your meal, let's drift over to the lounge, see if the barkeep knows anything."

"Sounds good," answered Bill as he scooted his chair back.

As they approached the lounge area, they observed a bearded brute of a man behind the bar gingerly polishing glasses. He was dressed as if in Seattle or Portland, wearing jeans, a red plaid flannel shirt covered somewhat by a stylishly finished brown leather apron.

As they sat down on the barstools, Bob commented, "That's quite a shine you're putting on those wine glasses."

The Bar Tender responded as he held one up to the light, "Yeah, these Terri cloth rags seem to work the best... Gets the lipstick off," as he held it in front of Bob.

Bob nodded, "looks pretty good," as he watched the process continue - off the bar - wipe down, look into the light, put on shelf.

"Guess we'll have a bottle of beer," suggested Bob as he glanced at Bill.

Bill agreed with a nod.

As they got their drinks, Bob asked, "Just wondering if you'd seen anyone unusual coming or going over the last few days?"

"No, just you two," the bartender chuckled.

"Just kidding," he continued. As he reached across the bar to shake hands, "I'm Ted, Ted Wesley."

"Just joking around about the glasses," as he turned, took them off the shelf and placed them in the deep sink. "I like to study people's faces... Gets a little boring around here at times."

Both let out a small chuckle as they shrugged it off.

Bill eased a glance around the room and noticed some guys looking directly at him, then found his beer to be the center point of his life at the moment.

"Well," Ted continued, "there have been some folks in here recently that I didn't recognize nor could I tell you what country they were from - definitely foreigners, maybe middle eastern - Ordered their drinks but didn't seem to have anything to talk about... mostly just mumble to each other."

Bob glanced over at Bill, "That's interesting."

"As a matter of fact, there were three in here this morning. One of the local boys followed them to a hangar on the backside of the airport where they got in a mostly black helicopter marked Shasta Mining. They headed out northeast. Not sure where they could be headed to but no one around here knows of any new mines out that direction."

"Not a lot out to the northeast for sure," mentioned W.B.

"We'd better finish up this beer and get some sleep," suggested Bob.

"I agree," said Bill, "besides, don't we have a conference call at 2100?"

Bob nodded yes quietly.

They stood and reached across the bar and shook hands with Ted.

"Thanks Ted," Bob continued, "Have a good night. We appreciate the information."

"No problem. Good Luck out there," answered Ted.

As they both headed up the stairs to their rooms, "I'll alert Captain Tom," mentioned Bob as he glanced toward the bar.

They both cautiously continued to their rooms. Bill took a quick look over his shoulder before entering his.

Coming up on 2100 hours, Tom, in his deep underground apartment at Red Devil, hooked up his phone to the remote antenna system outlet and alerted all the pilots to check in.

All picked up at 2100 and signed on.

Captain Tom began, "Evening men. Hope all had a decent meal and in position to get some good rest tonight."

All checked in the affirmative.

So far, reports relayed today have reflected nothing positive with the exception of Bob and Bill's information from the bartender in Bethel.

"Mike..., anything today? Where are you by the way?" asked Tom.

"I'm at home actually, in my cabin right here in Napakiak, just down the river from Bethel," he answered.

"Some of the guys I've spoken to here have heard that there's been more than usual helicopter activity in the distance out to the north... thought I'd head over in that direction in the morning."

Wild Bill, Bob, what's your input on that?

"Well," Bob commented while reviewing his charts, "I'm thinking that if Mike's correct and with the information we got from the Logan House bartender, there may be a perceivable pattern here.

I'm thinking we should fly an arc around the west and northwest side of Bethel and work our way over toward Buck's route in the morning," he concluded.

"OK. That looks good on the chart whereas, Jerry and I will work between the Yukon and Kusko rivers and continue toward Bethel, mentioned Tom."

"Sam, your input...?"

"Been pretty quiet around these parts. We'll leave the Holy Cross area and continue to follow the Yukon, check the villages and continue toward the northern peninsula areas," answered Sam.

"Ok men, we know where Charlie's not it seems," Tom continued.

All the guys knew what he meant.

"We possibly could have an interesting day tomorrow."

"Any questions?"

No response.

"Ok, AM Brief at 0700".

"Bob out." "Bill out." "Jimmy out." "Sam out." "Jerry out." "Buck Rogers, Pilot Extraordinaire - Out."

"Tom - Out," as he ended the phone call. He dialed the Colonel immediately.

"Colonel Bill, just checking in... All aircraft are accounted for and on the ground for the night."

"Anything so far?" asked the Colonel.

"We have only rumors at this point and a few comments from some of the locals primarily around the Bethel area."

"We're planning to continue to work over toward the Bethel Peninsula tomorrow."

"Jerry and I are at Red Devil. Bill and Bob are in Bethel getting the floats on as we speak. Sam and Jimmy are on the ground at Holy Cross.

Mike is in Napakiak just south of Bethel and plans to work toward the north northeast in the morning.

"Sounds good Tom. We should have both engines on Mother by morning as well. As soon as we get the go ahead from maintenance, we'll be headed on up your way."

"OK Colonel. If we don't find anything tomorrow in those areas, we'll converge over toward Unalakleet for tomorrow night."

"Each of the guys have their GPS Tracking Devices handy and will reinstall them at your call," concluded Tom.

"That would be good for us and very good for your guys if you get into any trouble. Weather should be clear along the coastal area tomorrow and should hold for at least 24 hours. Who knows? Maybe someone will get lucky tomorrow and find something. Thank your guys for doing a thorough job out there. I'll let you know when we're on station with 'Mother' tomorrow."

"Will do Colonel... I'll check in at 0715," concluded Tom.

Deep in thought he closed, carefully folded and pressed his satellite communications equipment into his backpack.

He removed his Glock holster and hung it on the bed headboard, pulled out the weapon to make sure it was ready and reinserted it into the holster.

Stripping down to his johns, he climbed into the comfortable bed and settled in for a good night's sleep.

CHAPTER 18

RECON - DAY TWO

November 11, 2011

6:45 A.M.

After a restless night's sleep, Mike checked in early..."Good morning Captain Tom."
"You're up early Buck," stated Tom.
"Been up for a while, laying out some grid lines for today... Just noticed," as he glanced at his calendar, "It's 11-11-11...How about that - Could be my lucky day."
"Anyway, it was pretty quiet around here up until about three o'clock this morning. Heard something fly over my cabin but couldn't identify the sound. I hustled outside, just caught a glimpse, more or less a silhouette of a helicopter - no running lights visible. He must have had some kind of suppression system, about as quiet as some of our military - seemed to head north from here."
"Sounds pretty odd," Tom responded.
Mike continued, "I made a mental note last night and plan to head that way this morning then back over toward some of the coastal villages. Like to get an early start."
"Thanks for checking in Buck. Sounds good... Let's get our conference call going. The guys need to hear this."

7:00 A.M.

Conference call check in –

All were suited up, had charts laid out and were ready for departure as they checked in for the morning briefing.

"Good morning men," called in Tom.

"After your reports last evening, it seems we've pretty much covered all the villages and areas along the Kusko and have pretty much covered the Yukon from Holy Cross north with no real results."

"If you'll look on your maps, one of the areas not yet covered is the area north and northwest of Bethel and also further out on the peninsula toward the coast."

"At zero three hundred, Mike witnessed a low flying helicopter headed north - northwest in that general direction. It was blacked out with no running lights."

"I checked with base ops and they've assured me there are no operatives in the area."

"Any activity in the area immediately north of Bethel would be somewhat unusual because if you look at your charts, that's pretty much volcanic terrain and that out to the west along the coast, there's a major Bird Conservancy area."

"In that light, our plan for today is to converge from different directions into that general area."

"As you know, we now have two aircraft on floats that will begin working along the coast."

"That will be Bob and Bill."

"Sam, Jimmy, why don't you head the furthest north of our search quadrant up to but remain south of Hooper Bay and Chevak. Then work your way down the coast then inland from Hazen Bay and work a north south search pattern working to the east."

"OK here," replied Sam. "OK," agreed Jim.

"Wild Bill, Bob," Tom continued, "Head south, down river, then work your way west and up and around the coast line to the Ninglick River and then east into the Baird Inlet. Scan those shorelines and when low on fuel proceed direct to Bethel."

"One of you possibly land up at the old Newtok Seaplane base and check things out there."

They both looked at their charts carefully and agreed.

Tom continued, "The Company did some research per our projected routes and it seems the village of Newtok has been abandoned due to coastal flooding and I imagine the Seaplane base has been shut down as well."

"Basically, see if anybody's home there at all and if so, see if they've heard or seen anything unusual."

"Jerry and I will head more or less directly toward Bethel and work some grids to the north."

"We're on channel 1477 HZ today, 377.711 VHF. Your squawk code when 'Mother' shows up is 7375. This could possibly be our lucky day."

"Any questions - comments," asked Tom.

There were none, so Tom, in conclusion, "Although, we're definitely Recon only, just due to the fact that we're possibly closing in on a hornet's nest, make darn sure you're armed and ready for anything."

"Gentlemen - Good Flight!" he concluded.

"Bob out." "Bill out." "Jimmy out." "Sam out." "Jerry out." "Mike, alias Buck Rogers, Pilot Extraordinaire - Out."

"Iceman - Out," as he clicked off and then dialed the Colonel to report readiness and their plan

8:00 A.M.

After stowing their phones, all grabbed their gear and headed toward their waiting aircraft.

Most of the men had a partner to confer with, were deep in the Last Frontier and happy to have the privilege of serving their fellow man again. It wasn't the same for Mike.

A now thoughtful 'Buck Rogers' seemed to hesitate leaving his small cabin home.

He dropped his gear by the door, then walked back and sat for a moment on his quilted bed, glanced around his one room cabin looking at some various Alaska memorabilia, keep sakes and aircraft pictures, then zeroed in on some family pictures on his mantel.

He stood, sauntered to the mantle, and touched the face of his kids and of each person. He then glanced just to the right and saw his military dog tags hanging on a rusty nail. He carefully lifted the chain off the nail and placed it around his neck.

As he walked by his small cracked mirror, he turned, saluted, and smiled... "Ohhh Boy!" then reluctantly stepped out and pulled the door shut.

After a short walk to the airstrip, a quick recheck of his aircraft, arms and ammo, he climbed aboard, belted in, ran a quick checklist and turned the key bringing the Cessna 206 to life.

After a good warm up and run up and with no one else around, he taxied out onto the dirt strip. He glanced back again at his cabin by the water, then looked straight ahead.

"I have the need... I have the need for speed!" as he applied 10 degrees of flaps and eased the throttle forward.

"Show me what you've got baby!" as he pushed the throttle to full, then clicked it to the left and forward to max.

A dust cloud formed behind the aircraft and after an extremely short ground roll, he rotated and seemingly exploded into near vertical flight through 5,000 feet.

"Whoa!" He rolled it upside down to stop his climb, then rolled out level in a turn toward the north.

Settling into a cruising altitude of 5,500 feet, he departed the Bethel area on his planned route in the general direction of the night flying helicopter.

"Iceman- This is Buck," he checked in on freq.

"Short delay... Forgot something at the cabin," he stated and continued,

"I'm on the trail of the helicopter... just cleared the Bethel area."

"Sounds good Buck. All the guys have checked in and are headed along their routes toward our convergence area," concluded Tom.

"See you there," Buck concluded.

9:35 A.M.

The Colonel checked in with Captain Tom, "Iceman, this is Mother."

"Hello Mom, what's for lunch?" "Disregard"... "Men... All patched in?"

All answered, "Buck" - "Bear Man" - "Wild Bill" - "Jimbo" - "Bagman" - "Sampson."

"Captain, we're a hundred out of Bethel and plan to join up as soon as possible. All systems are working and we're on the prowl this morning," called the Colonel.

"Also, just in case we need some folks on the ground, we have aboard 27 of Alaska's finest, an elite team of Eskimo Rangers heavily armed and ready to jump."

"Sounds good Colonel... Not familiar with the term Eskimo Rangers," inquired Tom.

"They're an Alaska National Guard reserve unit, made up of highly trained and skilled Alaskan Natives of various ethnic groups... Used to be called the Alaska Territorial Guard or ATG during WWII... Reorganized a couple of years after 9-11 and became an active unit about five years ago. They're Special Forces Trained and most were born and raised in Alaska," concluded the Colonel.

"Sounds like some good guys to have along," Tom concluded.

"Gentlemen... Chips in please," called Tom as he pulled his GPS Tracking Chip from the small lead based container. He then inserted it into the panel.

As all complied, they began to appear on the Colonels screen aboard the Super DC3 as named, green targets complete with altitude, airspeed and vertical speed readouts.

With the terrain clearly defined he could see where each aircraft was and could direct or warn as needed.

"Back to your troops aboard Colonel... How did we rate getting the National Guard involved?" asked Tom.

"I guess we have a mutual friend, this unit's Company Commander... Lieutenant Colonel Robert Weston, said you and he are Blood Brothers and he still owed you one from a long time ago," answered the Colonel.

"Said he had a planned training mission this week but thought he'd let his troops come along with me instead just to get some in-flight training experience," he concluded.

"That's pretty awesome... I'll have to look him up when we get back to town," answered Tom.

As the mission proceeded into its third day, all were vigilant and carefully watched for any sign of activity.

"Iceman, this is Buck," Mike called.

"Go ahead," Tom answered.

"I have a lone mountain in the distance about my 11 o'clock at about 40 miles... Could possibly be the destination point of the helicopter if my estimated track is correct."

"I'd like to continue toward the mountain if ok on your end," he inquired.

"Sounds good Buck. Remember to keep good distance - Recon only."

"I'll keep you posted Captain," Buck answered.

<u>10:07 A.M.</u> - Wolf Creek Mountain Area:

As Buck approached the mountain, he began a slow descent and planned his flight well to the right of the mountain hopefully to appear to anyone there that he was passing by.

For a time, he observed nothing unusual.

"Ice, this is Buck. No activity so far. I'd like to slowly descend back around the mountain and get a closer look."

"Ok Buck," Tom answered.

Buck peeled off his route and headed toward the peak of the mountain where he planned to begin a slow spiraling descent down and around the mountainside.

In close now, looking at every nook and cranny, he suddenly spotted an unusual shape - a cave like dent in the mountain side. He moved away from the mountain side and returned for another look.

"Ohhhh Boyy.....," as he broke the silence.

"May have something here Iceman."

"Just found somewhat of a cave indent on the side of the mountain."

"Continuing around the mountain at 1,500 feet..."

As he rounded one of the rock outcroppings, "Whoa!!!, Two black helicopters sitting at what looks like an old Village Site just northwest of the mountain."

"Buck, maybe you'd better move on out of there and let Mother analyze the situation," called Captain Tom.

"OK, will do. I'll plan to depart and leave about where I came in," answered Buck as he left the helicopters.

Continuing, still with no apparent activity on the ground, he continued around the mountain.

As he proceeded to about the point where he first began his spiral around the mountain, now at about 1,000 feet, he again spotted an unusual pattern on the hillside below, "Here's a pattern. Looks manmade - almost like a terrace."

He began a turn around and as he looked closer, he could see what appeared to be an old sled dog trail leading from the terraced area toward the cave or tunnel he'd seen previously.

Looking more carefully now with half flaps down he continued to survey the hillside.

"Change my angle," as he pulled the nose up and over.

"There it is... a camouflaged airstrip! I'm looking right at it. The runway is the exact color of the other terrain."

"Buck, best get the heck out of there and wait for some backup," Tom said urgently.

"Ok, Will do... Leaving to the north."

The Colonel checked in, "What's the length of the airstrip?"

"Looks about 3,000 feet," Buck answered.

"No problem for us to land if needed," the Colonel commented.

As Buck made another turn toward the airstrip, "Guess what! Now there's a CASA Aircraft sitting at the end of the field with engines running. Where'd he come from?"

"Holy cow! There's a large flat hangar at the end of the strip. Was invisible from above but now I can see the open doors."

"I'm going to fly on by and hopefully appear to depart toward the north," concluded Buck.

"Buck, this is Jimbo," I'm seven miles out and plan to stay away from the mountain but converge with you on the north side."

"Sounds good Jimbo. I've got you on TCAS," Buck answered.

Sam checked on, "Buck, Jimbo, this is Sampson. I'm coming up on your location 10 miles out."

"I have a visual on the CASA that has just departed your location. It appears that he's on a beeline for the coast."

Sam continued, "I'm in position to follow him and will keep a few miles in trail."

"Keep him in your sites Sampson," requested Tom.

"May just be a mining crew heading to Bethel," he continued.

"Buck, this is Iceman."

"I'm coming into the area as well, but I plan to hang out around 7,000 feet for a few minutes to see if any other aircraft depart or show up."

"Hope everyone's 'TCAS' is working well... Gettin' to be a lot of birds in the sky."

Colonel Bill checked in, "Iceman, since the runway and hangar were camouflaged, my feeling is that at the very least, there's something illegal going on down there."

"Also, we've got two more primary targets now off the mountain, probably the helicopters... Doesn't look like they're headed for Bethel but directly toward the coast."

"We'll follow up at the mountain, but perhaps you and 'Bagman' should head on over to the coast in trail as well."

"Bagman here... I'm about 30 southeast of your area and would like to finish my last grid line here, then swing over Nelson Island and catch the Ninglick River northbound and hook up with Bear Man and Wild Bill," Jerry called.

"Roger that Bagman... No problem... Sounds like a good plan," answered Tom.

Tom continued, "Colonel, this is Iceman... I'd like to hang out here at the mountain, keep an eye on my guys for a few minutes since you're still a ways out."

"Roger on that Ice... No problem here," answered the Colonel.

"Any hostile actions?" the Colonel asked in a general broadcast.

"Nothing from any of our guys yet Colonel, but really has the feel of a covert operation of some type," reported Captain Tom.

"Okay. Keep us posted of any sign of a hostile action," the Colonel requested.

"Will do Colonel. Iceman out," answered Tom.

All double clicked their mikes to keep from clogging the airwaves.

The Colonel continued, "Remember guys, you are reconnaissance only. OK to take a look around but utilize all safety precautions. I have informed Galena and Elmendorf as well as the Navy that we have activity in this area."

10:15 A.M. – Newtok

Captain Wild Bill, in his newly reconfigured Cessna 206, after finally hearing some radio chatter from the Colonel's Super Three, decided to check in, "Mother, this is Wild Bill."

"Just coming up the river toward Newtok and the old seaplane base... How do you hear?"

"Loud and clear Wild Bill. We've got you both on our screen, answered Colonel Bill.

"And, just to advise, we've got several primary targets coming in your direction. Looks like their ETA is approximately 45 minutes."

"You'll be looking for a CASA cargo aircraft and two black helicopters. Sampson's in trail. Bagman's converging into your area as well."

"Have you seen any kind of landing strip in the area?" asked the Colonel.

"Nothing apparent so far, but we'll keep an eye out. It would help if you can keep us updated on their route and estimated time," answered Wild Bill.

"Just got a good hit on your CASA and helicopter traffic. They're at about 500 feet AGL with no transponder codes - looking at 38 minutes to your location."

"Have you stopped in at the seaplane base?"

"Bear Man's just touching down as we speak," answered Bill as he banked left and glanced down to see Bob just now skimming the placid water.

A moment later, he was leaving quite a wake which meant he had landed.

As Bob slowed into a taxi on the water, "Wild Bill, Sounds like you're in touch with Mother."

"Yep... We've got a very nice set up for communications. As far as we know, it's totally in house with no one else able to listen. There's a time delay but Iceman hears everything through Mother as well," Bill answered.

As Bob idled the aircraft and settled into the water, he continued toward the dock, "Doesn't look like anyone's home. Buildings and homes look abandoned. Lots of erosion near some homes but many standing. All look empty."

"I'll ease up to the dock and take a better look around," as he taxied into the dockside perfectly, pulled the mixture shutting down the engine.

With hardly a ripple, the metal of his left float gently bumped against the dock piling.

Looking carefully, he eased his right hand onto his Glock lying on the seat.

Smoothly lifting it, he rotated it, checked for a full magazine, then slid it into his shoulder holster.

He reached behind his seat and pulled his M16 forward but kept it low so as not to expose his firepower.

Quietly, he opened the latch on his door, pushed it open and stepped onto the float.

Quickly placing a rope on the clevis, he listened carefully. With apparently no one around, he stepped up onto the old wooden dock.

Now, with his 16 at the ready, he approached the small building sitting on the dock.

As he entered the unlocked building, he found nothing but scattered bits of paper, old oil cans and other trash.

Speaking into his mouth piece, "Bear Man here - The fuel shack is empty. The dock's not maintained very well. The village appears to have been abandoned."

"I do however have a feeling I'm being watched," he concluded.

"Bear Man... Better get back in the air... Let's try to meet up with the folks coming down the river... Find out where they're going," suggested Bill.

"Sounds good Wild Bill. I'll be up in a minute," Bob replied.

He watchfully walked quietly back toward his aircraft. As he stowed his weapons, he again felt as if he was being watched.

He stepped out onto his float, untied the line and pushed off from the dock. As he climbed into the pilot's seat, he again subtly scanned the tree line.

With nothing noted he started the engine and began an idling water taxi to the main stream.

As he was about to reach his takeoff point, off to his left he noticed a white spot on the water near the edge of the grassy shoreline.

As he got closer, he realized it was cigarette butts, apparently looking as if an ash tray was recently dumped in the water.

"Wild Bill, this is Bear Man."

"Go ahead."

"Looks like there is someone covertly standing watch in the area - evidently a smoker. Just found some sign. Going to continue to depart as planned but we better keep this location in mind."

"Will do and I'll pass that on to the Colonel."

As Bob cleared the dock area, he eased the throttles forward, lifted off and headed to join up with Wild Bill.

CHAPTER 19

BUCK AT WOLF CREEK MOUNTAIN

10:21 A.M.

"Iceman, this is Buck."

"Go ahead."

"I've flown around the area now three times and haven't seen a soul move. There's no other aircraft that I can see anywhere."

"This possibly could be some type of drug and alcohol operation and that was the operators that fled the scene."

"Could be sophisticated enough that they have radar or some type of surveillance that saw all of us converging in the area."

"I'd like to land and take a look around if that's ok with you and the Colonel."

"You possibly are right Buck."

"Any problem with that Colonel?"

"No problem from here. We'll be overhead the mountain in approximately 20 minutes," he answered.

"Jimbo, why don't you land as well to give him some back up on the ground. I'll remain in orbit for some eyes in the sky," concluded Tom.

"Will do Iceman," answered Jimmy.

Buck quickly checked his weapons, did his final landing checks, turned and made a full flap short approach onto the dirt runway on the opposite end from the camouflaged hangar.

"Wow, nice compacted runway!" as he completed his very short roll out.

He turned toward the side of the runway, pulled the mixture and rolled off between some small trees.

He rolled to a stop, quickly exited the aircraft and with weapons and pack in hand, moved into some thick underbrush.

With his Glock and knife secured on his hip now, he carefully removed some grenades from his pack and distributed them around his belt.

After taking another good look around with binoculars, he slowly stood, took a deep breath, flipped the safety off his M16 and began walking along the tree line toward the hangar.

Glancing over his shoulder, he saw Jimbo's 206 on short final.

Jim landed, rolled out and exited the runway and his aircraft in the much the same fashion.

With his M16 in hand and grenade launcher slung over his shoulder, he ran in a low crouch to catch up with Buck.

They proceeded to the hangar and with full military protocol entered. After a quick search of all the spaces they found no one there.

"Iceman, this is Buck. ... Hangar's empty - Quite sophisticated though. Looks like a full sheet metal shop, engine shop and avionics lab."

"Are we sure this isn't some NSA outpost or something?"

The Colonel answered, "I'm running all that through the channels. I'll keep you both updated."

Jimmy and Buck left the hangar and proceeded up the small road leading around the mountainside.

After about one-quarter mile on the steep, winding dirt road, they came onto an apparent mine with a large steel door blocking the entrance.

"Found a locked steel door covering a mine entrance or the mouth of a natural cave," called Mike.

"Jimbo, Buck, this is Ice. I can be there shortly if you would like to hold up."

"Totally quiet around here Iceman... We can knock the lock off and take a quick look inside and hopefully solve our mystery."

"Proceed on. You're probably right about no one being there if the door is locked. Just watch for booby traps."

Jimmy came forward with a small C4 charge.

"Where'd you get this Jimbo?"

"Oh you know"... Sam's armory."

After molding the small charge around the lock and inserting the detonator, they quickly stepped around a large boulder.

Jimmy pressed the remote button.

A bang! and as the dust began to clear, they saw the lock was gone.

Waiting for a moment at the ready, they crept forward and put their shoulders into the large steel door.

As the door slowly opened, they stepped carefully just inside and were in view of a very large cavernous room with concrete floor, walls and ceiling.

Another cautious step inside... then, they both stood there stunned.

"This is bad news. Captain! THIS IS VERY BAD NEWS!" called Buck.

"You won't believe what's in this mountain!"

CHAPTER 20

DISCOVERY

"Iceman... Looks like a small version of an IBM sitting on a pad looking out the top of this mountain. Must be about 50 feet long and appears ready for launch."

"There's some steam or smoke coming from the base... Nobody around... Not sure what's up but better get some rocket folks in the loop like right now."

"Colonel, this is Iceman... Did you copy that report? Better get some 16's in the air!"

"Elmendorf... Code Red Flag! ... We need some backup at Wolf Creek Mountain and Top Cover in a block of airspace to cover the entire Bethel peninsula," the Colonel called urgently.

"Guys, I'm plugging all of you onto the military channel for coordination," he continued.

Buck and Jim quickly and actively looked for any clue about the missile.

Jimmy climbed a ladder onto the first layer of scaffolding, discovered a door off to the side and entered into a small room.

As he looked around the room, "Buck! Found a control panel on the second level... Waaaa-yy...too complicated for me."

"Thought you were pretty sharp on electronics," yelled Mike.

"Sharp possibly, however everything is in a different language!" responded Jimmy.

"I'll see if I can shut it off until the troops get here," as he pulled the main circuit breaker next to the panel. Nothing happened.

"I've shut off the power but the panel's still alive!" he yelled as he frantically searched for a way to disconnect it.

Realizing that there must be another power source running the system, he got back into the control panel, "Found a timer of some sort... I can read that... Shows 23 minutes!"

"What do you think? yelled Mike. Is it going to launch?"

"My guess... It definitely is!" he yelled back and continued,

"I don't know what it is but we've got to shut this thing down."

"Iceman, this is Buck. Over..."

"Iceman! This is Buck. Over."

"The mountain is blocking our radio!" he yelled to Jimmy.

"We've got to stop this thing ourselves!" he concluded.

Jimmy climbed up another level, looked around and saw a lever to extend a catwalk to the nose of the missile.

Grabbing some tools from a table nearby, he jumped on and extended the walk out to within reach of the nose cone.

"Let's see what you've got in here," he said softly.

He tapped and looked at options to get inside.

Finally he found an entry point, removed the panel and exclaimed, "Oh no. Oh my God! It looks like a Nuke!"

Buck charged up the metal scaffolding and onto the cat walk.

As the warhead came into view, "Jim... It's a dirty bomb."

"This is going to kill a lot of people... Innocent people."

Thinking for a moment...Jimmy concluded, "Well if we can't shut down the missile launch, we can at least get this stupid bomb out."

"Grab that bag of tools over there Buck. Let's get this thing out of here."

They both worked frantically, removing screws and cutting bolts and wires.

Finally it was loose. As they pulled to lift out the 18 X 24 inch device, they realized it weighed well over a hundred pounds. They continued to struggle until the deadly device was lying on its side on the catwalk.

"Captain Jim," asked Buck, "You up to carrying your half to the plane? We'd better get it out of here before someone realizes what we've done and what we have."

"If it goes off here with the 10,000 foot winds at 75 knots from the north, should just about wipe out northwest Alaska. Where do you suppose this thing's aimed?"

Jimmy looked at his compass then up at the opening in the mountain," I believe Anchorage and Elmendorf!"

"Let's get out of here," yelled Jim as he lifted his half of the warhead.

Mike, with the strap, shouldered his M16 and grabbed his half.

As they finally made it down to the lower floor and the base of the missile, "Wait a minute! Sit this thing down for a moment," yelled Jimmy.

Now on the main floor of the launch pad, Jim ran to the wall, grabbed a sledge hammer, turned and slammed each of the rear fins several times... "Should throw it off course, but now we have no idea where it will end up."

They continued to struggle with the bomb, exited the cave entrance and turned down the roadway toward the airstrip.

Suddenly, the mountain began to rumble.

Buck, "There she goes."

As they sat their burden down on the ground to catch their breath, the rocket slowly exited the camouflaged mountain top with a deafening roar.

As Buck and Jimmy continued to clumsily jog down the small road toward the airstrip and their aircraft, Buck yelled into his mike, "Hey boys, loose missile coming off Wolf Creek Mountain."

"We've disarmed it... we think...! Took a small Nuke out of the nose cone."

"We've got it!" yelled the Colonel as he saw it come onto his screen.

"Superman, Superman... Are you up?" the Colonel called for the F16 Squadron leader.

"We have disabled the warhead but the missile has launched and is headed south... looks out of 3,000 feet... Any chance you can take it down?"

"Super Man's three minutes out," he answered.

"Coming your way Iceman!" shouted the Colonel as he viewed the course and trajectory of the missile on his screen.

"Iceman, looks like from here you should head east or west..." continued the Colonel.

"Yeah, I've got it," answered Tom.

"West it is," he called as he entered a 60 degree bank steep turn and powered into JATO.

He tightened up in the turn as he passed two G's at 200 knots.

"Ice!... It's turning with you... Converging...!" yelled the Colonel.

"What the heck...? Is it tracking me?" as he went to idle power, rolled into a steep turn to the right back toward the East and hit his JATO power again.

He grunted out... "Talk to me Colonel."

"It's locked on..." as he looked at his screen. "Doesn't look like you're going to outmaneuver it at the moment," answered the Colonel.

"Ok...," Tom called as he went to idle power and turned to face the relentless oncoming missile head on.

As he rolled out level, "I'll try to stay out of the way of this thing, go vertical or something when it's on me... With the relative speed, I feel like I'm in a hot air balloon today."

"There's actually a bright light on the front of it!" called Tom.

"Guess I am its target now ... Seems a little erratic but still coming my way."

"Sure is," called the Colonel as he viewed his screen. "Coming straight at you... accelerating."

"May be some type of cruise missile with a tracking device that's locked on to your aircraft," stated the Colonel.

"Yeah, this is not good," Tom stated as he squeezed on the yoke and began moving his aircraft left and right like a pendulum in an attempt to confuse the missile's tracking device.

He was keeping the light directly on the nose, testing his rudder and aileron coordination, getting ready for a timely move in the right direction.

"Ice'... I'll do the countdown," continued the Colonel. When it's on you, I'll give you the computer recommendation to break right or left. No guarantees though... Looks like you've got 27 seconds."

"Thanks, I'm all ears here," answered Tom as he stabilized his aircraft with eyes glued onto the light of the oncoming missile.

"Black Widow... Black Widow, This is Superman" called the F16 squadron leader... We'd like to take out that missile but we're still two minutes out at Mach Two plus."

"Would you kindly take out that missile before it hurts someone?"

"Take it out with all prejudice!"

"Gladly Colonel," came the answer in a soft woman's voice.

Suddenly, a horizontal shock wave appeared at about 10,000 feet above Iceman's aircraft. Two seconds later, out of the induced cloud, dropped a Black Space like Jet Fighter of some kind.

Then from the craft shot an extremely violent supersonic barrage of what seemed like extremely fast pulses that disintegrated the southbound missile. Not only did it disintegrate the missile, the blast continued its force to the surface carrying all the debris with it.

"All prejudice delivered, "in the woman's voice again.

Tom was shaken and speechless.

Then, as he shook off his shock of being alive and in one piece..., he quickly turned to look for the black jet, "What the heck was that?"

"That's me," as a black F27A7 with a female pilot dropped into slow flight on Tom's left.

"Wow..." as he looked left and viewed the unusual looking, partially invisible, black craft.

His gaze quickly went to the cockpit where he could clearly see the profile of a lady's face below the brow of her black, wired up helmet.

"Well..." Thank you Mam'," Tom said gratefully.

She looked over and smiled broadly, "Glad to be of service Captain Tom."

"Oops, Time's up... Going back where I like it best," as she eased over to his 10 o'clock position, eased the nose upward, then hit her pulsating afterburner quickly vanishing from site.

Tom leaned forward to watch her simply disappear in vertical flight.

He sat back, reached forward and shakily tested his controls and turned on the autopilot.

"Whoa," as he tilted his seat back somewhat and reached for a bottle of water.

He'd only had a moment to recompose, when, "Ice - This is Buck," called Mike.

"Go ahead Buck," Tom replied.

"You won't believe this.

"We evidently woke up some troops... Must have been in a safe house for the launch somewhere under the mountain."

"They're just coming by the chamber entrance and firing our direction," he called loudly.

"We're at the airstrip, just about to our planes. This Nuke is heavy and pretty awkward. Jimbo and I are running out of steam... Any help out there?"

"Ok Buck. Hang in there. The Dragon is pretty close by. Should be there at any minute."

"We're on it," called the Colonel.

As they closed in on their aircraft, Jimmy let his end of the Nuke down to the ground and spun around firing several rounds toward the pursuing terrorists, "I'll hold these guys off from here, just get in your plane and get the heck out of here. Can't let them get this Nuke back."

"You sure Jimmy?

"I'm sure Mike," as he grabbed more munitions from his airplane.

"Those maniacs will detonate the Nuke right here if they get their hands on it!"

Buck lifted the heavy Nuke onto his aircraft step, pushed the right seat completely back and lifted it onto the seat.

As he began to secure the warhead with the seatbelt, he heard a beep coming from another part of the Nuke. Rotating it slightly, he quietly pulled his Leatherman tool from his pouch, then with his Philips head, carefully opened and raised another panel they'd missed before. He didn't say anything about what he saw.

He quickly secured the door, turned back to Jim who was hustling toward better cover and shouted, "Good Luck my friend."

"Dang," he said quietly as he belted in and started his aircraft.

He began to taxi out but glanced back catching Jim's view, saluted, then taxied away at a high rate.

Not planning to slow at all, he continued to increase his speed toward the runway. As he neared the end of the runway, slipped in full throttle and with his rudder, slid his aircraft to align with the runway. He advanced the throttle, energized his JATO system power and literally launched off the runway into vertical flight.

"OHHHHHH.......Boyyy! Love doin' that!"

The adjacent sky was filled with tracer rounds but none were hitting their mark.

As he rolled out level at 5,000 feet, he mumbled to himself, "I'll just head down toward the coast, drop this baby in the ocean and let the Navy deal with it later."

"Jimbo... Hang in there," called Captain Tom as he continued toward the mountain. "Should get some help soon. 'Mother' should be here momentarily."

"There's a lot of 'em. Still coming around the mountain!" called Jim.

"Wonder if they would have stayed in their cave if they knew that Mother was and still is a Dragon!" asked Tom.

"I'll let her tell them herself. Gotta go now..." Jimmy yelled as he hurriedly moved toward better cover.

The firefight continued as the first wave of terrorists closed in.

"Jimbo, this is Mother... Coming up on your six," called the Colonel.

Jimmy glanced behind him and heard the low flying rumble of the big Super DC3 engines.

"Keep your head down for a minute. I'll see if we can get them off you for a bit," as the large aircraft rolled steeply onto its side exposing the dual .50 caliber Gatling guns.

"After this pass, I'll drop Alaska's finest Calvary right behind them," as he glanced back at the hooked up and standing troops. They'll help you clean this mess up," concluded the Colonel.

Jim hustled further up onto the hillside and dove for better cover behind the rocks.

As the terrorist troops charged his position they began to riddle his area and aircraft with holes.

His aircraft exploded into a large fireball.

Jim looked back momentarily, rose and fired angrily on several very close troops, then heard the Gatling start up.

He dove again for deeper cover as the steel rain began to consume everything in its wandering path.

After one pass, the ship leveled and seemingly turned away. Then, troops wearing all white wing suits began streaming from the aircraft, all turned in formation and headed directly behind the perceived enemy lines.

Within seconds their chutes began to pop open very low to the ground and precisely behind the terrorists.

***

Buck, once back into cruise flight, flipped the beeping panel open again and saw that indeed the countdown had continued on what was a warhead and now was a bomb.

"Iceman, this is Buck."

"Go ahead."

"Got the package heading toward the coast, however, got another backup timer active now showing 19 minutes," Buck said disgustingly.

"Must be a backup in case the missile were to malfunction," answered Tom.

"Think you can shut it off?" asked Tom.

"I'm working diligently trying to find something," answered Buck.

With his autopilot on and a GPS course to the nearest shoreline, he continued to dig into the wiring and components.

He'd pulled his survival mirror from his pack and with it; he discovered another hidden switch deep inside the wiring.

Carefully, he flipped the small toggle switch with his Leatherman tool screwdriver and stopped the countdown... again.

The timer stopped at 6 minutes 57 seconds.

"Whew!"

"You ok Buck?" asked a concerned Tom.

"I'm good... Timer's stopped - Should be able to get to the drop point."

"Jimbo getting some help from the Colonel?" a concerned Buck asked.

"You bet. He should be ok. Troops are on the ground, however, his plane's in shreds."

"How about you Iceman?

"Well, back in business, just coming up on Russian Mission heading your way."

"Bagman's swung south toward Newtok to hook up with Bear Man and Wild Bill. Said he had a feeling they were headed for trouble or that trouble was headed toward them."

"Wish you could have seen that missile take down," said Tom.

"Did see it. Got a quick look when that horizontal shock wave hit about 10,000. It was quite something... looked pretty darn close to you," answered Mike.

"Well close enough to give me a splitting headache," said Tom.

"Iceman, this is Colonel Bill. There's a possibility that you may have a concussion and may need some medical attention."

"No... Just a headache," he replied.

"OK... My Psych is just a little... out of sync here."

"You won't believe what just happened," he continued.

"I was very nicely focused on the light of that giant cruise missile, personally after me by the way, preparing to shake it off at the last second, when...

A girl - flying a black, mostly invisible, Mach Seven F something or other, just dropped out of space, and blew up with 'prejudice' I might add, a Mach something IBM, then... stopped by to say hello and see how I was doing sitting here in my hot air balloon 206."

"And, with some kind of wicked pulsating afterburner, she went vertical and into space somewhere," he concluded.

The Colonel chuckled, "Captain Tom... Welcome to the future."

Notice the wiring on her helmet? he asked.

"I was close enough to see that," Tom answered.

"It's a smart helmet and I understand it only works on the female pilots. Guess we don't use enough of our brains to qualify."

"I think I know, but why do they call her Black Widow," Tom asked.

"Well... She's hidden until needed, drops in on her prey and as you can see has a super gun aboard. Some kind of Gatling sonic laser combo with shrapnel flying through it."

"If she'd not passed back below the sound barrier a mile above you, she would have torn your aircraft to shreds just from that alone."

"You're probably thinking about deceleration and G's I'm sure... but, you'll have to catch her at the club. You've got a Top Secret Clearance. She'll be happy to talk technicalities," the Colonel concluded.

"This is Superman," called the F16 squadron commander. "Don't feel bad boys. We had not seen a demo of the craft or the weapon until six minutes ago - Adds another meaning to Shock and Awe."

The Galena F16's had arrived on site and had begun to survey the situation while they coordinated with the Colonel.

"Good morning Colonel... Captain James Anderson, USAF, Call Sign - Superman... Got here quick as I could."

"Excellent... Thanks for coming to the party!" replied the Colonel.

"Anything particular at the moment? Kinda looks like things are under control."

"I believe they are Superman. However, might want to provide us a little top cover for a bit."

"Will do Colonel," as they reformed their formation and climbed out.

"Understand one of your guys has the Nuke and is heading toward the Sea."

"That's affirmative. He should be about 35 miles from Wolf Creek Mountain by now," answered the Colonel.

"This is Buck... That's correct. I'm north of Marshal now westbound at 5,000 feet," interjected Mike.

"Should be coming up on the mud pots shortly headed for open water," he concluded.

"I'll be your wingman Captain Rogers," stated Captain Anderson.

Captain Tom interrupted, "This is Iceman... Actually, it's Captain Land, Captain Michael Land."

"Ok Captain Land... I'm 18.3 miles on your six. Be there in a couple of minutes and I'll fly cover for you to the coast."

"Appreciate that. Sure don't want any more surprises today," he replied.

"Superman, you can call me Buck now. I may not answer to anything else."

"Ok Buck. I'm high, have you in sight and on your six at three miles," stated Superman.

"Thanks," answered Mike as he looked around and spotted the closing F16.

"Iceman... This is Buck," called Mike.

"Just wanted to clarify my mission and goal for the tape."

"Go ahead Buck," answered Tom as he clicked on the recorder.

"As you know, I've got a nuclear bomb in the right seat of my aircraft, heading toward the coast."

"I should be at the drop point in about 18 minutes if this baby will hold together at 200 knots."

"I plan to fly out into the Norton Sound seven or eight miles, push it out the door, where hopefully it will not detonate but sink to the ocean floor for the Navy to recover it. I'll make sure I log the exact GPS coordinates."

"I hear you Buck. We've all been flying along by the seat of our pants so to speak. Thanks for getting that on tape."

Tom asked, "Colonel, while we have a few minutes, would you propose a question over all our frequencies to see if anyone has any better options at this point?

"Be advised," Mike pointed out, "We're at the three count on shutting this thing down. We've been successful for the third time. The timer is now off but sits at 6 minutes 57 seconds."

"And Iceman, remember, as you always said, respect the Alaska Aviation Rule of Three. Three times and you're out or you better get out! Trouble is... I don't have anywhere to go. Can't really go back to the barn," he concluded.

Silence...

"Colonel?" came the questioning voice of Captain Tom.

On board the Super three, the Colonel looked around at the several technicians and crew members on their phones and monitoring their screens.

They all gestured and shook their heads, 'We have nothing.'

As he completed a short conversation on the phone with the Elmendorf Control Center, "Ice, Buck," this is Colonel Bill. "Sounds like the only option at this point and all have come to the conclusion that it's probably not the best but the only plan at this time."

"It shouldn't detonate when it hits the water but should sink rapidly to the bottom for Navy pickup."

"We have a Seawolf Class submarine steaming toward the coastal rendezvous point. They have a recovery team aboard and will modify their course as soon as they get the coordinates," he concluded.

"Sounds good Colonel," responded Buck. "I'll let you know when I cross the coastline - Should be in about nine minutes.

Meanwhile, back on Wolf Creek Mountain, Jim slipped up on three surviving terrorists, "Freeze!"

They turn and fire.

Jim lets go with his M16 dropping all three. Then silence.

He carefully approached the men and rolled one of them over and searching, found no identification.

"Iceman..., this is Jimbo... Short fire fight on the ground here. These guys are definitely not from around here... Look Middle Eastern... No I.D..."

"Terrorists for sure," replied Tom.

"Jimbo... When you get in the clear, would you take another look around the launch tunnel and see if you can find anything," Tom asked.

Ok will do," as he noticed troops in white approaching his area.

"Captain Tom, Top Cover, this is Colonel Bill."

"The Eskimo Rangers have reported all under containment at the mountain. They have a few prisoners with six wounded. They also have 23 civilians that were kidnapped and evidently forced into labor.

"Roger that," replied Tom.

The Colonel continued as he viewed his screen, "What we're seeing here is that the CASA aircraft and helicopters are approaching the Newtok seaport area, possibly intending to land at another camouflaged airstrip there.

Looks like Sampson's about four miles in trail. Probably has them on TCAS."

"We might want to head that direction ourselves Colonel," answered Tom.

"I agree," the Colonel answered, then directed all aircraft to head toward the coast.

"Sampson here - I've been maintaining radio silence closely in trail. Have a feeling they might have some listening equipment aboard."

"Thanks Sampson. We could easily take them out but there's a chance of hostages aboard, so just remain in surveillance mode," called the Colonel.

At 10 miles out, the CASA aircraft flanked by the two helicopters approached the Newtok area. On final descent, the flight crews checked in with their hidden contact on the ground.

Subsequently, a crew of men on the ground began dragging large amounts of brush away from a hidden airstrip adjacent to the sea plane dock area.

In the electronically sophisticated aircraft cabin are the leader and several members of the terrorist group.

All had been watching the Terrorist Commander's laptop computer screen looking for the expected strike on their target 350 miles south at Elmendorf Air Force Base and the adjacent city of Anchorage.

They had trouble tracking the missile but had estimated that it was a computer glitch.

The only other aircraft they had seen in the area was Buck Rogers' Cessna 206.

Chapter 21

TROUBLE FROM BELOW

"Ice, this is Bagman," called in Jerry as he approached the Newtok area from the south.

"Go ahead Bagman," Tom replied.

"Coming up the river south of Newtok... about 10 miles," he answered.

"Roger that. Keep a close eye out for a possible landing strip in your area," Tom answered.

"Will do," answered Jerry.

As the terrorists closed in on their landing point, one of them looked at his watch and back at his screen.

"Commander... no detonation..."

The terrorist commander glanced at his screen, quickly opened his brief case and pulled out a small black device. "We activate the Bomb from here."

"But Commander, we do not know where the Bomb is," his second in command shakily stated.

"Doesn't matter," the Commander said sternly.

"Where ever it is, it will be totally devastating to all of Northwest America. Winds aloft...-", he checked another screen – "are now at 87 knots out of the north northwest."

He continued to type in the code then pressed the red button on the device.

He laughed a demonic laugh afterward and called out loudly, "Say goodbye to your women and children you stupid Americans."

***

Suddenly a beep came from the cabin of Buck's plane as the Nuke's timer re-energized.

Buck spun around and saw the timer counting down from five minutes.

"Iceman...!" he called loudly on the mike.

"Go ahead Buck."

"Remember that timer we completely disabled twice...?"

"Yeah, I do."

"Well, it's running again.... They must have had an integral failsafe backup system."

"It just came alive! Shows 4 minutes 30 seconds now. I'm still 6 minutes from the coast and 7 minutes from the drop zone even with max thrust!"

He pressed on the auto-pilot and began to work frantically on the timer.

"Not working," he mumbled.

"Can't take a chance of an airborne detonation here," as he considered that several villages and the city of Bethel were not far off from his flight path.

"Gotta' get this plane on the ground... In a canyon... in a lake.... Gotta' get down! Got to get down!"

He hit 'Terrain' and zoom on his G3000 and took a close look at the upcoming terrain as well as what was behind.

He saw a small mountain range he was familiar with and pushed over to get a better look as he dove toward the surface.

"Iceman... Remember that old Russian mining area about 20 miles north of Mountain Village?"

"I do Buck... Seems we landed there a few years back, nothing around but some interesting ruins," answered Tom.

"Remember that vertical mine shaft about 30 feet wide and we estimated it to be close to 2,000 feet deep by throwing big rocks in it?" asked Buck.

"Sure do."

"Well, I see that mine shaft."

"It would be great if you could drop it in... Not sure what the result would be, but it should be better than a surface or airborne detonation. Think you drop it or land and drop it?

"Well....," as he moved the G3000 navigational joy stick to the mine entrance, "calculated to be about three minutes till there."

"Glances at the Nuke, "Timer just passed three minutes forty seconds."

Buck pressed on the already full throttle looking for additional power.

Suddenly and solemnly, Buck spoke into the mike, "You know Tom, Guys...It's been a heck of a ride hasn't it."

"You're not going to make it are you Buck..." Tom asked solemnly.

"No way I can land, roll out, get this thing out of the aircraft and drop it in."

"Would just detonate on the surface... Take all of us out and everyone throughout most of western Alaska and the Yukon Territory."

"Wish I could've dropped it in the drink... Just too far away."

"If I can do this right, it may tear up Mountain Village pretty good, probably St Mary's as well; Bethel should only get an earthquake.

"Yeah, Buck" came back Tom as he looked at an old chart, "How're you going to do it?"

"Tom, there's no way I can fly and bombardier out the side door and hit that hole in the ground - Can't afford to miss this one."

"Going to begin a Split-S... fly the vertical leg, but not pull out of the dive. If I do it right, I'll enter the shaft in vertical flight and shed the wings at the mine entrance which should explode my fuel tanks. The way I figure it, from there, I'll have tons of dirt following me down the shaft, hopefully to seal off the mine - Should contain the bomb."

"Buck, there's got to be another way!" Tom said in an anguished voice.

"No. Captain Tom. This is the only way I can see that we can contain this stupid thing."

He reduced the throttle and began to slow his aircraft as he continued to descend now within three miles of the mine shaft.

"Tom, you and the Good Lord helped buy me a year, two months six days and ...," as he checked his watch, "nine hours of life bailing me out of Seattle. You'll never know what that meant to me. Plus, I think it all happened for a reason. I was meant to be here at this very minute."

"Now to be able to contribute this to my friends and to my beloved America means everything to me."

He continued as all was quiet on the radio waves, "... and Tom, if you come out of this ok, would you stop in at my place in Bethel, pick up my pictures and personal stuff and take them down to Anchorage?

"Sure will Buck," answered Tom.

"Tell my wife, I still love her. Check in on my kids from time to time. I would appreciate that."

"Ok Buck, I will and I'll check on the kids. You're a good friend, a 'Pilot Extraordinaire' for sure... and one of the best friends Alaska and America has right now."

"Gentlemen... Best all leave the immediate area," Mike concluded.

Captain Anderson of the F16 group checked in, "This is Superman... We're gonna' give you about 50 miles Brother.'

"Thank you for your service to our country!"

"Group full afterburner - Point Bravo... Engage."

All the F 16's in the area hit afterburner and departed the area.

Buck continued, "There it is... Looks perfect" as he gazed at the open mine shaft.

Buck again glanced to his right at the timer showing 1 minute 30 seconds.

'Should be perfect,' Buck thought to himself as he gazed toward the shaft.

"See you on the other side you old warrior," Tom concluded.

"Yeah, Captain Tom, it's been good to know you."

"If you'll excuse me for a moment, I need to speak to someone privately."

"Tom away." as he banked sharply and hit full JATO system throttle.

Buck turned on the autopilot briefly then bowed his head for a moment in silent prayer.

He looked back up, ensured he was at the right altitude and airspeed.

As Buck approached the vertical mine shaft entrance, he removed his headset and slapped his face twice on both cheeks. He can still be heard over the speaker.

"Gentlemen, I've been told to let you all know that Captain Michael Land will be successful in this endeavor and he is ok to go," as he eased back the power slowing the aircraft further, then selected full flaps.

The bomb's timer was now below one minute showing seconds and counting down rapidly.

'Focus Michael....'

From the guys prospective, Buck's voice calmly spoke into his mike in a professional voice, "the timer now at 30 seconds... - a little pitch up 80 knots... 75 - 70 - 65 knots... roll her upside down," as he went to full right aileron and kicked in the right rudder, "out the bottom... got to hit dead center."

He precisely adjusted the controls and power, then manually added more trim which helped with the control pressure.

The mine entrance rapidly closed on the windshield.

He hit the vertical mine shaft entrance dead center and shed the wings with an explosion.

As the fireball appeared at the mine shaft entrance, Tom called out, "He's in the shaft!"

In a darkening cockpit free falling in his wingless aircraft, "Never saw an altimeter unwind like this."

As the blurry instruments now were showing minus 1,000 feet, he began jerking left and right. His wingless aircraft banged on the sides of the shaft pressing in the fuselage of his aircraft.

He banged his head right then left, then suddenly came to a stop as tons of dirt and rock piled onto his destroyed aircraft.

With the gleam of the panel lights shining on his face, "I did it!" he shouted.

Sitting for a moment in triumph, "Dang... Didn't go off..." "Guess they're just gonna' have to dig me out of here now."

He sat in silent contemplation as blood trickled down his face.

"Ooooohhhhhhh Boyy! What a way to go..." He shook his head and grinned.

White Light...

From the surface - The surrounding ground rose 30 feet, then fell, sending a concentric seismic shock wave that passed rapidly across the Yukon River spilling it over its banks and continued to roll across Mountain Village and St Mary's dropping most of the houses to the ground.

As it continued across all of northwest Alaska, Bethel received a short lived but radical rolling earthquake.

"What was that?" asked a worker at the Bethel airport.

"Oh, just another earthquake I suppose," said a close by mechanic.

"Sounded more like a sonic boom to me," said another.

"Capt Tom... Status...! Capt Tom... Status!" called Colonel Bill from Mother... "We're 30 out,"

"Bomb's destroyed below the surface. Buck's down," answered Tom as he gazed at the huge dust cloud.

"Sorry for your loss Captain," answered the Colonel.

"Yes... He was a certainly a great friend of mine... And to anyone on frequency, Michael Land, alias Buck Rogers, Pilot Extraordinaire' just took care of the Nuke destined for Anchorage... Gave his life for his country."

"Moment of silence please," he asked.

After a few moments, "Thanks Gentlemen. Doesn't look like there's any chance of fall out... Now just a small dissipating dust cloud. Quite a shockwave though... Probably going to hit the seismic charts in Anchorage for sure."

"Colonel," Tom continued. "We've got two birds down. The rest of us are headed out on the peninsula toward the coast to see if we can catch up with Sam and the CASA."

"Bear Man and Wild Bill on floats were last reported near Newtok... They may be faced with some serious problems as well," Tom concluded.

"Thanks Tom," the Colonel replied. "I'll swing back and land at Wolf Creek, pick up Jimmy and a few Rangers. Be down there shortly."

Tom took another glance at the new crater and dust cloud.

"Good Bye Buck... We'll get those guys," Tom concluded.

A couple of more thoughts of Buck, then he banked sharply left toward the coast and eased his throttle forward to full JATO system power.

CHAPTER 22

BOB AND WILD BILL AT NEWTOK

Bob and Bill continued to work together on their way up the meandering river northward as they searched for any possible landing strip for the CASA and helicopters.

"Bear Man... Looks like there's been some activity over there by Olor Island," called Bill... "Can you see the snow machine tracks just south east of the Island?

"Looks like maybe some Ice Fishermen. I'll check it out," answered Bob.

"I'll take a look up the valley to your right," answered Bill.

As Bob approached the island, "Two snow machines came out of a large camouflaged dome on the frozen shore of the island."

"They could be hunting as well - Just not sure. I'll plan to keep a little distance," commented Bob.

He continued to fly a wide circle and began a descent for a little better look.

The men turned back toward their tent and then back toward the circling float plane, stopped and began to wave frantically.

Having rescued several folks before, Bob complied and drifted back to over-fly and check out their situation.

"Wild Bill... Think I'll go in for a closer look. They're waving ... Looks ok from here. They may possibly need some help," called Bob.

As he approached, the men suddenly pulled automatic weapons and began firing heavily.

Several rounds struck the bulletproof windshield and as Bob banked to turn away, they concentrated their fire on his door and side window.

The shooters, as they realized the pilot was protected, focused all their fire on the fuel tanks and pontoons. As he completed his turn away, they reloaded and focused all their fire on the tail section.

"I'm hit!... I'm hit!..." as his cockpit filled with smoke and the aircraft began to shake.

Fighting for control now with a badly damaged rudder and elevator, he continued north to follow the partially frozen river.

"Gotta put her down Wild Bill," he yelled into the mike.

He continued to struggle to stay in the air to put some distance between himself and the pursuing snow machines.

"OK Bear Man... I see a flowing part of the river, bearing about 30 degrees, just on the other side of the shoreline hills. Looks like about four miles. If you can make it there, I'm high now, but, I can come in right behind you, land and pick you up," Bill called.

As he heard two thuds on his aircraft, he glanced out the window and down at his left pontoon, "Can't stay down long though, just got a couple of holes in my left float."

"I see the stretch of water you're talking about," called Bob as he continued to descend toward the possible landing area up the river.

Suddenly, a "Crack"... "Creak"... as his left pontoon began to separate from the aircraft.

"Wild Bill!... Not getting in the water... Gotta' pontoon problem!"

"Whoops," answered Bill.

Bob continued, "Looks like a... kinda flat area along the right shoreline. I'm heading down there, maybe you can land on the water. I'll land and unload some of my stuff."

As he approached his landing spot, he shut off the fuel, turned off all electrical and tightened his life jacket.

Closer in now with only the sound of the wind and with the left pontoon now further detached, he cautiously applied the manual flaps.

With full flaps set, as he approached touchdown, Bob expertly held the damaged left pontoon a little higher than the right. He touched the right pontoon softly onto the snow covered ground, then held the left one off as long as he had lift on the wing.

The wing dropped, the left pontoon separated and the left strut began digging in.

"Oh no... Not again!"

Violently, the aircraft flipped completely over tearing off the left wing, then slamming the tail.

"Crack!... then Thud!..." as the tail hit the frozen ground.

After a short forward slide, the completely destroyed aircraft came to a stop... Upside down.

As the dust cleared, he took a quick status of his limbs, hands and head. "Hey, I'm good."

He realized, that once again he hung upside down in his seatbelt and shoulder harness.

"Ok... I know this..."

He carefully detached his shoulder harness, released the pressure on one side, then pulled the harness belt to full extension. Then he wrapped it around his wrist, tensed his body, released his lap belt and with a heavy grunt, swung around, landed on his hands and knees on the ceiling now floor of the aircraft.

"Oww!" as he unwrapped the belt from his wrist.

"At least I didn't land on my head this time," he stated quietly.

As his two front doors were buckled from the impact, with the fire extinguisher in hand, he began to slowly crawl through the mangled aircraft toward the back door.

As he felt the tunnel vision effect and with perceived darkness closing in, he stopped for a moment, closed his eyes and laid flat.

As the adrenalin shock began to wear off, with eyes still closed, he suddenly picked up the beautiful sound of a Cessna 206 engine idling and then pontoons as they skimmed on the surface, then slipped along in the water.

Bill had touched down on the icy river and had begun to slow as he approached the river bank nearest Bob's aircraft crash site.

As he read the nearby currents near the rocky shore, Bill positioned the aircraft to let the right pontoon ease up to and touch onto the more pronounced downstream rocks.

He left the engine at idle for a moment, then, ensuring he was set in the current perfectly with no movement of the aircraft, he shut down the engine.

With pistol in hand, he eased out onto the left pontoon... All was quiet. Then he holstered his weapon and took a quick look back at the bullet holes along his float's water line.

As all appeared to be holding, he opened the pontoon storage, quietly eased out the anchor and tossed it onto the muddy ice strewn river bank.

Expecting the worse, he listened intently as he wrapped the anchor rope on his pontoon clevis.

There was no initial sign of life, just silence.

He grabbed a fire extinguisher out of the pontoon storage compartment and jumped onto the river bank.

As he scrambled toward the crash site, he was somewhat relieved to hear a door or windshield being kicked hard, then saw the windshield pop out.

Bob, after he had struggled to get to the back, after recovering somewhat, had realized the back doors were bent as well as the front doors and there was no way to get out so he had returned to the front.

There was no other activity for a moment. Then, Bob's arms appeared through the small space.

As he cleared the wreckage, he turned on hands and knees, reached in and continued to drag out all the weapons he had shuttled forward.

"Need anything Bob? You okay?" Bill called in a loud whisper.

"Yeah...," still with his back turned, "Do you know if this should go in my logbook as a Float Plane landing or land plane landing?

"Couldn't say," as he glanced at the upside down destroyed aircraft.

Bill shook his head and turned as he realized Bob was generally ok.

On the run, he called, "Don't mess around here too long... I don't hear them yet, but they may be able to get over here.

Bill trotted back toward his aircraft and found it still sitting stable in the light current. Quickly down the bank, he threw the rope off the pontoon clevis and quickly climbed aboard.

After a quick mental checklist, Bill started the engine.

He sat for a moment to ensure the aircrafts right pontoon was still resting against the rocks and stable.

He then left the engine at idle, pushed the right seat back down, climbed into the back and quickly unlocked and flung the side door open.

As Bill climbed back into the pilot seat to be at the ready, Bob quickly arrived and threw his survival gear bag, some weapons, including a grenade launcher and ammo into the back.

Without hesitating, he jumped aboard and slammed the door shut.

"Bob, did you remember your peanut butter jelly sandwich?" asked Bill as he began to power up for taxi.

"Already ate it!" yelled Bob as he latched the door and began to evaluate his weapons.

"Best get a seat belt," Bill called back as he eased the throttle forward and drifted further away from the rocks.

Bob quickly sat down and snapped on his seat belt.

"Belt's on!" shouted Bob.

"OK! We can go!" shouted Bill.

Bill continued to move the throttle forward as he lined up with a somewhat crooked and short section of the flowing river. As he came into best possible alignment, he pushed up to full throttle, engaged the JATO system power, touched some protruding rocks, then practically leaped out of the water.

"Hey, getting pretty good at this," Bill exclaimed over the engine noise as he cleared the trees and banked to the right.

"Yeah, me too!" as Bob looked back at his crumpled up heap of aircraft parts on the ground.

"Let's head on up the river and go around that bend. They'll think we're running..." requested Bob.

"Well, we are supposed to be running!.. But..., we are supposed to take pictures too," agreed Bill.

As he pulled the camera from under the right seat and tossed it into the back, "Here's the camera. Guess we've got to go back," yelled Bill above the engine and wind noise.

"OK! I'll get the shots, you fly the aircraft," shouted Bob.

"You know Bill," as he unbelted and climbed up between the pilot seats, "They shouldn't have shot me down... Makes me pretty ill," Bob said firmly.

Bill glanced over his shoulder at Bob and noticed the bloody bandage on his left forearm and wrist.

"Well... Remember Bob... Recon only... We're supposed to get out of here and call for support you know," answered Bill.

"Don't worry, I'll give you support from the back seat," as he began to pull several weapons to within reach.

"Sounds good to me. Need anything on that arm?" questioned Bill.

"No... I'm good... Let's go," answered Bob.

He then picked up his grenade launcher and began to load it.

He pulled the left rear seat shoulder harness down, connected it to the seatbelt and looped the modified restraint around his upper right leg.

As they continued their climb out heading up river, he reached and opened the rear door, "Oops, door popped open." Then with a screwdriver, unscrewed the hinges, loosened the door and with a 90 knot wind whistling by, detached it and carefully pulled the large door inside the aircraft.

"Gonna get cold in here!" chirped Bill.

"Let's give them about three minutes, then turn around, kick in the afterburner and we'll come back around and let them have it," suggested Bob.

"With that door off, better get your vest on. Most of the aircraft is bullet proof but I don't think the pilots are," stated Bill.

"You're right about that," answered Bob as he reached into his survival gear bag.

"Better report.... I suppose... maybe get some backup," said Bill as he found and put on his headset, then tossed a headset back to Bob.

"Ok Bill... I'm on line and vested up," called Bob a moment later as he had put on the headset and finished securing his Kevlar vest.

"Bob, you do the talking. I'm pretty busy up here," called Bill as he continued to fly low following the meandering river and simultaneously studying the terrain on the G3000.

"Iceman, this is Bear Man and Wild Bill here on the same rodeo... I mean radio," called Bob.

"Go ahead Bear Man," answered Tom.

"Well, we ran into a little trouble here just north of Newtok... Got shot at, actually, well, actually, I got shot down... lost my aircraft."

"Wild Bill has picked me up and we're planning to head back down river to survey the situation and see who did the shooting," Bob concluded.

"Good grief Bear Man! You okay?" Tom asked.

"Just a few bruises but still here," he answered.

"Bill took a couple of rounds in one of his pontoons," as he peered out at the bullet riddled left pontoon, "but the rest of the aircraft seems to be holding up ok."

Tom replied, "Good. Glad you both are ok."

"We're all on our way to rendezvous in your area, however, we do not believe you have any assets near you at the moment," Tom concluded.

The Colonel broke in, "Estimating 15 minutes to your location."

"Sounds good. Thanks," answered Bob.

"The bad news is, especially for you two," continued the Colonel "is that there's a CASA aircraft and two helicopters less than five minutes of you.

"We have every reason to believe they are the leaders of this incursion and are headed to a concealed airstrip somewhere," concluded the Colonel.

"Sure could use that Gatling camera," remarked Bill.

"We haven't taken any action on them simply because we do not know if there are hostages aboard," stated the Colonel.

"OK... Hope to have something for you shortly," answered Bob.

"Look out!" Bob yelled into his mike. Bill quickly rolled hard right and deviated from his flight path to avoid a collision.

"That was close... Just passed head on with a low flying aircraft... looked like a CASA - Seemed to be heading straight to Newtok!"

Wild Bill continued in his turn to follow and keep them in sight.

Sam called, "Wild Bill, this is Sampson... At your six, 500 above, in trail of the CASA and two helicopters."

"Thanks Sampson... If you've got them, we have some unfinished business over toward Olor Island... strictly Recon of course," answered Bill.

"Sounds good Wild Bill..." as Sam flew by on their right side.

"Noticed your passenger door was removed - Looked like Bear Man was at the ready with some long range camera devices."

"You bet... Looking for some good shots," Bill concluded.

Bob grabbed the camera, waved at Sam and held it out the door.

"See you boys. Good luck," Sam signed off and went to JATO system power. He quickly caught up with the CASA aircraft and disappeared from sight.

"You ready Bob?" asked Bill as he began his approach toward their targets.

"You bet Bill," answered Bob.

As they cleared the last hill and entered the flat terrain of the frozen lake, the two snow machines came into sight.

The armed terrorists heard the oncoming float plane and turned to meet them head on.

"Bob... I'm going to get within about a mile, hit full JATO power, go right over them, pitch up hard, roll right and go to full flaps which will put the sun at our backs and leave you a clear line of fire. Sound okay?" stated and asked Bill.

"You bet... I'm ready," answered Bob as he double checked his made up harness system, tightened his vest and checked his M16.

As planned, Bill slipped the throttle forward to full JATO system power and accelerated rapidly.

Rounds began to pepper the windshield to no avail as Bill passed 180 knots.

With full JATO power, he flew directly over the two at 200 knots plus, catching a spray of rounds impacting the bullet proof belly.

He immediately went to idle power, pitched up 30 degrees, rolled right and went to full flaps.

That combination quickly decelerated the aircraft as if he had slammed on the brakes. The turn set Bob up for clear shooting. The terrorists with sun in their eyes were totally missing their mark.

Bob quickly took out both terrorists with one of the snow machines exploding.

"Good shooting back there Bear Man," Bill called as he rolled out and began a gradual left turn to take another look.

"They're done. Would you make another pass over by the camouflaged tent?" asked Bob.

"Sure can... Same profile ok?" asked Bill.

"Works for me," answered Bob.

On this pass, Bob utilized his automatic grenade launcher, fired five rounds into the tent and surrounding area and left the entire area in flames.

As Bill began his turn back for a final pass, an explosion occurred which devastated the entire area.

"Must have had some heavier stuff down there," commented Bob as they turned away again and headed back south.

"Think you can reattach that door Bob... before we both catch pneumonia?" Bill asked.

"You bet..." answered Bob... "Guess we better get back down to Newtok."

Chapter 23

CAPTAIN JERRY BAGWELL

Coming up the river following Bob and Bill's previous Float Plane route, Captain Jerry Bagwell arrived in the Newtok area.

"Bagman here... Checking in at Newtok," he called.

"Good to hear from you Bagman," answered Bill.

We seem to have encountered some of the bad guys and have just went head to head with the CASA and two helicopters heading your way.

"OK, I'll be looking out," answered Jerry.

"What the heck? ... Wild Bill... I'm a little south over the river at 2,000 feet... Just spotted a wake but haven't seen any boats at all," called Jerry.

"That doesn't sound too good," answered Bill.

"Gonna' drop down and check it out," called Jerry.

As he got closer to the converging line of the wake, he saw the thin antenna of a conning tower skimming through the water heading directly toward the Seaplane dock at Newtok.

"Guys... I hate to tell you this, but it looks like a submarine coming up the river heading right to the village dock," he warned.

Suddenly, in the distance the three approaching aircraft came into sight.

"I've got the CASA and helicopters now as well," he continued.

"They appear to be landing somewhere close to the float plane dock," he concluded.

"I'm in a climb to get a better visual but plan to keep my distance for now," he reported.

"Copy that," called Tom.

Out of 3,000 feet, Jerry watched the arriving aircraft descending toward a point and finally spotted the small airstrip that had just been uncovered.

"We have an airstrip now," called Jerry.

"Bagman, this is Sampson. I've been in trail of the CASA and see the runway as well. It's about 50 yards from the float plane dock and parallel with the river."

"The landing strip must have been very well camouflaged for Bear Man and Wild Bill to miss it," Jerry commented.

"Probably hasn't been used in years and easy to cover up. Those guys seem to be masters of camouflage," responded Sam.

"I have a feeling this has been their pick up and drop zone all along and evidently their planned evacuation outlet," stated Jerry.

He watched the CASA aircraft and helicopters land with the CASA spinning around and coming to a stop in the center of the runway.

"Holy cow," called Jerry looking at the airstrip. "There must have been 15 people jumped out of the CASA, with 4 or 5 more getting out of each helicopter."

"Those are the guys I believe that planned and almost pulled off another 911," stated Sam.

"Let me get my camera," said Jerry as he fumbled behind his seat.

He pulled up his M16, "Guess this will have to do. I'll get their attention and maybe we can delay them till the cavalry gets here."

"Might not be a good idea. Looks like that sub's about to surface," called Sam.

"Sam. Did you see where they parked the CASA? asked Jerry.

"Sure did Bagman. They left it right in the center of that short runway... Probably don't want any company today," Sam concluded.

Both helicopters had landed to the right side of the strip, their crew and passengers were running toward the dock.

Laying his M16 aside for a moment, Jerry pulled out his long range binoculars to get a closer look at who they were.

"Sampson. I've got hostages... five... no seven... being lined up beside the CASA," Jerry called peering through his binoculars.

"You copying us Ice?" called Sam.

"Sure am Sampson," answered Tom.

"I think they're lining them up for our consideration not to have a full scale air strike," called Sam.

"I agree Sam. However, my guess is that they plan to blow the CASA as soon as they get out of range, just as they remotely tried to detonate the Nuke," continued Tom.

"Colonel. Are you up?" called Tom.

"Monitoring... but in agreement for no air strike at this time," answered the Colonel.

"Looks like everybody's running for the sub. Hostages are chained together around the left landing gear strut," Sam called.

"I can get those folks," he concluded as he reduced power to idle and began a rapid dive toward the airstrip.

"Sampson, this is Bagman. What's your plan," called Jerry.

"Simple... I'm lining up now for the runway... looks about 800 feet with a large bump in the middle."

"You're going to do a Leap Frog aren't you," called Tom.

"You bet... Piece of cake in this baby... Besides the CASA 212 is a short little devil anyway... Remember you and me practicing that maneuver after you had to jump over that bull dozer at the mine strip back in 83?" asked Sam.

"How do you know I really did that Sam?" Tom asked.

"That yellow paint on your tires kinda told the story plus it seemed to work in practice," answered Sam.

"Well, that was less than a 10 foot hop... That CASA tail is about 20 feet..." continued Tom.

"If you do it, I recommend you hit the top of the CASA wing slightly left of center away from the hostages... should clear ok," concluded Tom.

"Ok... That's my plan," concluded Sam.

Jerry broke in, "Guys, I'm going to make a pass at the sub, ping a few off their conning tower... See if I can slow them down a little."

"Ok Bagman. Thanks. Keep a good distance away if possible," answered Tom.

Jerry pulled back the power and began his shallow dive toward the submarine. As he closed in, he steeply turned to the right rolled out level with his M16 out the window.

In full view of the situation and with the submarine fully surfaced, he let go several rounds striking the conning tower and hitting two of the terrorists.

"I'll be there in five minutes Bagman," called Tom.

"You better watch those guys. I believe they have heavy weapons aboard," he warned.

Suddenly a rear hatch opened with two seamen appearing on the deck. They immediately ran toward a covered aft gun.

Meanwhile, Jerry had turned his aircraft around for another pass.

"Whoops," Jerry commented as he saw them unveil a 3"- 50 Gun.

He immediately pushed over and dove to the 'deck' avoiding the first round.

They reloaded.

"These guys are persistent!" he stated under his breath.

When he saw the smoke, he hit JATO system power momentarily causing the next round to pass behind him.

Back to idle now, as he slowed rapidly, he rested his M16 on his arm and dropped one of the gunners.

Two more had arrived to assist, pushed the dead gunner over the side and reloaded.

Jerry turned away, pulled up and again hit the JATO throttle.

In vertical flight now, the next round passed below him.

He then slammed his rudder full right and went over in a Hammerhead maneuver, pulled on full flaps and as he had spotted a landing area, dropped below the tree line, turned and landed in a small ravine just out of site of the sub.

He shut down quickly, grabbed his portable headset and moved into position to get a good view of the sub on the other side of the river.

As he pulled out his binoculars and gazed at the activity on the sub, "Bagman here, I'm on the ground, in position to spot for the 'Force, Mother, or whoever gets here first."

"Superman's here but holding until hostages are clear," called the F16 Commander.

Jerry looked up and saw the F16's in a delta formation, orbiting the area.

"Mother 10 minutes out," called the Colonel.

"Boys, this is Sampson. Gonna' try to get those hostages clear shortly. I'm on a two mile final." called Sam.

"Best I can estimate, that sub will be under water in five or six minutes or less. You can bet they're going to blow up that CASA as soon as they dive," called Jerry.

"That makes me feel a whole lot better Bagman! Thanks for that update... Sampson on a one mile final," called Sam as he increased his focus.

Chapter 24

THE LEAP FROG ^v

Sam continued to close on the narrow, very short obstructed runway. Rocks and trees lined the sides with the two helicopters parked in the only turnaround space.

"Wish I could have landed somewhere else..." he said aloud to himself.

"Iceman, the CASA flight crew very nicely left their aircraft lined up perfectly facing my final approach. Should be a piece of cake," Sam called.

"Focus! Focus!" he yelled to himself as he was within yards of touchdown.

He continued to call his actions... "Zero flaps"... "70 knots"... "60 knots"... "Stall horn"... "Touch down"... "Rotate - full flaps"... as he jerked the manual flaps to full and added some power.

"Leap Frog!!!" as the aircraft lifted off again, Sam zoom climbed momentarily in a very nose high attitude. Hanging on the prop, flawlessly he maneuvered his half flying aircraft main wheels to hit on the CASA wing causing him to bounce.

He chopped the power, lowered the nose and simultaneously raised the right wing slightly to miss the tail of the CASA, then pulled hard on the yoke adding some power to cushion his stalled out landing.

He again hit hard on the main wheels on the 200 feet of dirt runway remaining.

He immediately kicked the right rudder and ground looped the 206, dragging his left wing around.

He was surrounded by dust and falling debris and simply sat there for a moment. "Piece of cake," he mumbled as he pulled the mixture off, then magnetos and master.

"Good going Sam," Tom had watched the whole thing intently.

"Where from here? asked Tom.

Sam had already converted to his portable headset, "Bolt cutters in my survival pack... Cut the hostages loose... Grab one of those helicopters and get out of dodge," he answered.

"Bagman here... The last of the enemy have disappeared down the hatch, including the fellows manning the three inch gun. Looks like they're submerging!"

"Copy Bagman," answered Sam as he ran with bolt cutters in hand toward the hostages.

He arrived and immediately cut free the most fit looking guy and handed him the bolt cutters, "Cut the other folks loose and meet me at the first helicopter!"

Sam leaped into the first helicopter, scanned the gauges... "Just a modified Huey," he stated under his breath as he began flipping switches and winding up the turbine.

As he was spooling up toward lift off power, all the hostages arrived and clambered aboard.

"Let's see if this bird will fly," he stated as he rotated the collective to takeoff.

Jerry watched the helicopter lift off and turn away from the runway with the hostages.

"Good job Sam! Best put some distance between you and that CASA," he called.

Sam had just cleared the runway area when the CASA exploded into a gigantic fireball taking with it Sam's 206 and the remaining helicopter.

The entire area was engulfed in dust and smoke.

"CASA blew!" called Jerry as he scrutinized the situation looking for any sign that Sam's helicopter made it out.

Suddenly, the Huey careened out of the smoke into the clear with smoke trailing.

Jerry broke into a large grin, "Hostages are clear!"

Sam called on a crackling radio, "All okay here. Heading to Bethel."

"Glad to hear it Sampson," answered Tom.

"Superman, this is Iceman"..., How far out are you guys?" Tom called.

"This is Superman. We have a full attack about to commence within one minute... Recommend all stay well clear of the dock area."

"OK Superman... I've got one bird on the ground less than one half mile on the opposite side of the river," called Tom.

"Should be no factor. We'll watch for him," answered the F16 Commander.

Jerry checked in on that, "Been here before boys. My head is down."

"We're slowing out of Mach and should be there in a moment.... Estimating 30 seconds to target."

The sub had continuously been moving away from the dock and now was completely submerged.

"May be a little late on this strike. The sub has gone below the surface," called Jerry.

The F16's came into view, approached with blinding speed and let go with several barrages of rockets into the water at the docks. The violent explosions sent massive plumes of water hundreds of feet in the air.

As they pulled up Jerry watched with binoculars and strained to see any sign of contact.

"Nothing," he called frustratingly.

"Superman... This is Iceman. I'll take a quick look if you guys are clear," Captain Tom asked.

"We're clear Iceman. I'm afraid they're too deep for our missiles," he answered.

Tom quickly arrived overhead and began to survey the area.

"No oil slick... No debris... Sorry," he reported.

"Bagman... This is Iceman... Better get back in the air... Stay in trail of Sam in case he has any problems."

"Thanks for spotting and glad they didn't take you out with that three inch!"

"Oh... That was easy. Those guys were terrible shots," he answered.

"Just hate it that those murderous maniacs got away," he concluded.

"Colonel. This is Iceman. What's the status of the Seawolf or any Naval resources?" Tom called.

"Just got off the horn with them Captain. They're no help at the moment... Still 23 miles out," reported the Colonel.

"Slight chance at best to catch them at sea..." he concluded.

The airways were quiet for a moment.

"Sampson... Are you up?" called Tom.

"Sure am Iceman," Sam called from the black helicopter. "I'm enroute to Bethel with the hostages... Mechanically, all's fine here... You can free up Bagman if you'd like."

"Thanks Sampson. Great job," Tom concluded.

"Bagman... You can join up with us," Tom called.

"Will do," answered Jerry.

"Wild Bill...This is Iceman... How're you and Bear Man holding up?"

"We're ok here... Anything we can do?" asked Bill.

"Yeah... Let's form up and drift out over the water for a few minutes... Keep an eye out for any debris, oil, or any sign of the sub just in case the 16's did some damage," called Tom.

"Let's begin working at the mouth of the river, fly a standard fish spotting pattern for about 30 minutes, then head to Bethel for fuel. I'll take 2,500 feet," he concluded.

"Will do. I'll take 1,500," answered Bill from his Float Plane.

"I'll be there in about five minutes. I'll take 3,500," called Jerry.

"I'll join at 5,000," called the Colonel from the Super DC 3.

"Iceman, this is Jimbo... I'll join you at 5,000 feet as well," he called in a professional and very serious tone. "I'm in trail of the Colonel about nine... feet."

The Colonel turned and saw Jimmy on the mike at the rear of the cabin.

Finally, someone had gotten to the Colonel as he burst out laughing with all in the cabin joining in.

"Gentlemen... This is Superman. I can give you about 10 more minutes of top cover then we're headed home. Looks like a Navy problem from here."

The now deeply submerged submariner terrorists began to relax and celebrate what they perceived as a glorious victory.

They believed their attack on North America had been totally successful.

With sophisticated communication and sonar gear, they continued to navigate toward the open ocean.

CHAPTER 25

SURPRISE

Aboard the submarine, the Terrorist Commander gained everyone's attention, "All of you!"... This has been a great victory for our cause."
They all cheered and clapped.
He continued knowing they had intentionally sacrificed a hundred of their own men to complete their mission.
"This has been five years of hard work by the most skillful and dedicated men from our country. Excellent work by all of you!" he shouted.
Again they cheered and toasted each other with champagne.
As they toasted and continued to celebrate with music blaring in the background,
The Sonar man called out, "Captain.... Sonar Contact! Bearing 270 degrees... 500 yards! 450..."
All went silent as they gathered around the screen.
"400 yards!" called the Sonar man.
"This is impossible... Intelligence says their Seawolf Submarine is still 20 miles away!"
"Captain! Torpedoes!!! ..... Two!!... Four!!..."
He turned from his screen and looked at the Captain, then at the terrorist commander.

"Right Full Rudder! Heading 360 degrees! Full Speed ahead!" yelled the Captain.

"Dive... Dive... Dive..." he yelled loudly.

The Sonar beeps get closer together.

The terrorist commander and his second in command stared at each other as the crew and the other men began to panic.

Some screamed as the sonar blips got louder and closer together.

Then the twin multiple torpedoes impacted their submarine.

The underwater explosions were massive. And with a thundering eruption of the ocean surface, there blew a large plume of fire and water that continued hundreds of feet into the blue sky.

The sub obviously had been totally destroyed with all aboard instantly killed.

Captain Tom's aircraft was closest to the exploding geyser and was quickly enveloped in the water vapor cloud, smoke and debris.

The others immediately turned away to stay clear.

As they turned to look, most felt Tom's aircraft had been destroyed.

A moment later, a damaged, severely shaken Cessna 206 emerged from the thick cloud.

"Iceman?" the Colonel called.

"I'm here... Flying along in my Cessna 204... No make it a Cessna 203 as he gazed back with wind whistling through his broken rear windows," answered Tom.

"Did our sub take out those guys?" questioned Tom.

"No... The Seawolf is still 20 out," answered the Colonel.

"Colonel, this is Superman. We just flew over the sight and believe the explosion to be the terrorist submarine."

"There's nothing here for us. We may have damaged the sub and it may have simply blown up on it's on," he concluded.

"We're returning to base... Navy will be up in a while to search for survivors and salvage whatever remains."

"Superman... signing off," Captain Anderson concluded.

"Thanks for your help Superman," called the Colonel as the F16's formed up and made one more fly-by before heading to base.

Captain Tom called, "Colonel, Gentlemen, I'd like to orbit the area for a few more minutes, let the water settle down and see if I can spot any survivors or specific debris."

They continued in a wide circle weaving between the still remaining smoke, and watched below while keeping track of each other. The Colonel joined back up at the 5,000 foot level.

Suddenly the dark hull of a Submarine surfaced in Tom's 12 o'clock position.

"Everyone keep your distance from my position," called Tom.

I have a visual on another sub.

As a mysterious submarine craft of some kind surfaced Tom saw some very strange symbols and markings come into view.

"Well... Helllllloooooo," Captain Tom said quietly into his mike.

As the Sub totally surfaced, it continued to rise and to hover above the water!

Tom was dumbfounded!

A seemingly computerized voice came over the radios "Colonel Bill, Captain Tom and Team... this is Commander Traibe' of... Spirilla Monitor 7."

"I know you are surprised to see us and realize we are not supposed to be here, however, we've been listening to every transmission for days. Following your progress we have witnessed your valor and sacrifice as well."

"In that these terrorists were about to get away from you, we decided to end their submarine warring capabilities quickly and effectively."

"The base from which they came is in the process of being destroyed as we speak," he continued.

"Colonel, please give the following code to your Supreme Commander - Spirilla Monitor November Alpha Tango Oscar Sierra Mike 7. They will possibly understand why we engaged."

All listening were dumbfounded and without words.

As Tom continued around the 'floating Sub-like ship', he caught a glimpse of an obvious Captain figure standing in an open window. The 'Captain' saluted, then turned as the window closed.

"Navdi, Navdi, Navdi" ... was heard over the radio as the Craft descended into the water and disappeared.

Captain Tom returned the salute.

"Never thought I'd see this day," said Captain Tom.

"Me neither," said Jerry and Bill simultaneously.

"Did anyone else see that sub?"

All answered 'Negative'

"Who was it?" asked the Colonel.

"Well Couldn't really tell with the smoke and my crazed windshield." Answered Tom.

He realized he was the only one to actually see the Craft and said nothing further.

"You know gentlemen, I believe we will all wake up to a new day tomorrow," stated the Colonel.

"Looks like the military's here," as he looked at his screen at the multiple aircraft heading their way. "Let's head over to Bethel, regroup and see if any of us are needed elsewhere," the Colonel suggested.

"Sounds good, but, I'd like to make a quick stop at Napakiak, pick up some of Bucks things, plus I can fuel up there," Tom asked.

"If okay, I'd like to follow you over Captain," called Jerry.

"We would too," called Bill with Bob in agreement.

"No problem here. You've all gone way beyond the call of duty today," answered the Colonel.

As a matter of fact, if you would like, just continue on to Anchorage and I'll catch up with you there," the Colonel continued.

"Ok. Will do,' answered Tom.

Captain Tom said to himself quietly, "Only fitting Buck - We'll drop in to the last place you hung your hat. Maybe you left a few things I can take to your kids in Anchorage."

He turned and with Jerry now in formation and Bill and Bob down low in the Float Plane, headed toward the Napakiak village airstrip and Bucks home base.

Once settled on their trip, Tom took out a pad and jotted down what he'd seen and experienced. Closed his eyes for a moment, then drew a rough picture. He realized no one would actually believe him.

CHAPTER 26

MISSION ACCOMPLISHED

As the three aircraft traveled toward Napakiak, Tom tuned his ADF to see if he could catch a Russian radio station.

Suddenly, all the frequencies came alive.

"What's that blasted noise??? he mumbled.

"Bleep....Bleep..... Bleeeppppp."

The radio blared, "This is your emergency broadcast system.

"A shallow, 6.7 Magnitude earthquake occurred at 11:37 A.M. this morning. It was centered in the area 23 miles northeast of Bethel and has been followed by several aftershocks with an unusual 2.5 magnitude aftershock at 11:58 A.M. located 3 miles off the Bering Sea coast. Some broken windows have been reported in the Bethel area however no injuries have been reported. A possible Tsunami could occur anywhere along the coastline."

"Bleep....Bleep..... Bleep."

"This has been a broadcast of the emergency radio system."

The Radio Host came back on the air, "I've got Roger Smith from the Northwest Alaska Tsunami Warning Center on the phone."

"Mr. Smith... You're saying this was a very unique earthquake?" asked the host.

"That's correct Bill. None of us have seen a 6.7 magnitude earthquake emitted from 2,000 feet especially one not on any of our known fault lines? We're continuing to investigate."

Captain Tom smiled.

"Could it have been anything else?" the host questioned.

"Not really... Nothing that we know about at this time... We've warned folks on the coast to be alert due to possible tsunami conditions," Smith concluded.

Back in the Anchorage Seismic lab, James, a studious type person with large glasses, printed out the data from his computer, "Actually... looks like an underground nuclear test... He handed it to his supervisor.

The Supervisor remarked, "James! Do you really think the folks in Bethel are testing Nukes in their back yard," as he wadded up the report. They all laughed at his expense. He shook his head and went back to his computer. As they all sat back down, each began digging into their own results.

Quietly, the supervisor stepped into his office, opened up and looked at the report again, glanced over at the red phone and contemplated using it.

***

As they approached, Captain Tom scanned the south Bethel area as he studied his chart.

"Let's see, Buck said Napakiak was just downriver from Bethel and on the other side of the river."

"I have it in site now," he called.

"Jerry. Let's plan a left downwind entry for the south runway," Tom suggested.

Bill interrupted, "You guys don't forget... Bob and I are on floats. We would prefer to land on the water. Bob said they don't work out real well on land."

"Yeah. Might not be able to get fuel anyway," stated Tom.

"I think we're headed into Bethel, leave my aircraft there and fly down to Anchorage on the Three," Bill concluded.

"Sounds good Wild Bill," Tom answered.

"Jerry and I will probably head on down to Anchorage this afternoon. See you when you get down," answered Tom.

"Sounds good. See you later Iceman... Bagman...," Bill called.

"Wild Bill... Bear Man... Been one heck of a day," Tom concluded.

CHAPTER 27

LAST VISIT WITH 'BUCK'

Tom, with Jerry in trail turned into the traffic pattern at Napakiak, landed and taxied up to the fuel pump area.

John Sanders strolled out to meet them.

"Hello John... Buck Rogers sent us... Said this was the best fuel stop in the area," called Tom.

"You must be Captain Tom. Buck's mentioned you a few times. How's he doin?" asked John.

"He's doin' fine John... Not on this earth anymore," Tom answered.

"Sorry to hear that," said John thinking that indeed Beaver Fever finally took him out.

"While we're fueling, do you mind if I go over to his cabin?" Tom asked. "Buck wanted me to pick up a few things for his kids."

John pointed, "Cabin # 7 down by the river."

Tom didn't ask for a key since no one ever locked their doors out here. 'Why?' He thought... 'Everyone has guns... That's why.'

Captain Tom strolled across the field, then on to a small overgrown driveway leading down to his cabin by the river. The area looked much as Buck had described in one of his letters.

He arrived at Cabin #7 and as expected, the door was unlocked.

He slowly opened the door, entered the dimly lit cabin, felt for the light switch and found no switch. He then waved his arm around and felt a string hanging from an overhead light fixture, pulled it and turned on the light.

As he looked around, he observed maps, pictures of family, aviation books and other memorabilia.

In a small closet, he came up with an old suitcase and threw in it all the pictures he could find and anything he thought Bucks kids might want.

Scanning through the pictures, he came across one of Buck with Jerry and himself, smiled and placed it in his vest pocket.

He scanned around once more, reached for the light string but let it go.

He stepped into the door way and turned for a last glance.

"Buck!" as he shook his head and shut the door,

"Still leading the way," as he began to walk away.

"See you later on Brother," Tom closed. Old suitcase in hand, he headed up the hill toward the gas pumps.

CHAPTER 28

WARRIORS RETURN

"Captain, we're all fueled and ready to head to Anchorage," reported Jerry.
"One flight plan, two aircraft?" Tom asked.
"That's right," answered Jerry.
"OK. Let's go," Tom responded.
Under now overcast skies, Jerry and Tom took off from the small strip and headed to Anchorage.
The flight was quiet with both men still thoughtful as they approached the Alaska Range.
Suddenly Jerry pressed his throttle into JATO system power and pulled around Tom, waved his wings and began a descent.
"Bagman, where the heck are you going?" called Tom.
"Iceman, how about one more run through Merrill Pass for Buck Rogers - 'Pilot Extraordinaire'?"
"You got it! I'll follow you," Tom agreed.
As they descended to 3,000 feet and approached the pass, Tom began to remember some of the good times in their early Alaskan years.
'What an exciting time that was.'
The two flew further down closer to the ground as they entered the pass entrance. As they followed the main stream along, they had to quickly adjust right, then left to

get around boulders and outcroppings while calculating their next move in the rugged terrain.

Tom in trail of Jerry, watched his moves around the obstacles and for a moment visualized that he was watching himself somewhere back in time.

Both men enjoyed the sights, sounds and feelings as if reliving their early adventurous careers and feelings that went along with it.

As they cleared the Alaska Range, Tom announced, "That was for you Buck... and all the guys that have gone before us... Right Jerry?"

"Yeah... That's right," said Jerry.

Both contemplated what could go wrong and what had gone wrong for those guys.

Slowly, the lights of Anchorage came into view.

Captain Jerry in the lead picked up the Automatic Terminal Information Service first and passed it on to Tom.

"Iceman... Tango's current. Winds are three two zero at ten... Ceiling and visibility unlimited... Twenty nine ninety eight on the altimeter... Runway seven left,"

As they approached Anchorage International, "Anchorage tower," Captain Tom called, "this is November two one ex-ray, flight of two, 10 miles southwest inbound for landing with Tango."

"November Two One Ex-ray... Flight of two... Cleared to land seven left," answered the Controller.

They touched down one behind the other and on roll out, "Two One Ex-ray Taxi to parking," called the tower.

As they arrived at the hangar ramp area, they pulled in side by side in a military manner. They stopped, finished their shutdown checks and continued to sit with engines idling.

Neither pilot wanted to shut down.

"Open your window Jerry. Listen to those beautiful IO-580's..." mentioned Tom.

They both pushed their left earpiece back and sat with windows open for a moment savoring the sounds.

"OK...On my mark...three...two...one... Shut down," Captain Tom said quietly.

Both engines shut down simultaneously. They completed their shutdown checks, unbelted, opened their doors and stepped out onto the tarmac.

Both were quite stiff from the time in the air not to mention all the action they'd seen, yet they both began to inspect and wipe down their aircraft.

"I could sure use a shower and a good hot meal. How about you Jerry?"

"Sounds very, very good," he replied.

"Let's just head out. I imagine the rest will be here in the morning," concluded Tom.

"Who are those old guys limping around the 206's?" the lineman asked as he pumped gas into an aircraft on an adjacent ramp.

"Awe, Just a couple of retired airline pilots I think... up on a sightseeing trip."

"Yeah... Saw them come in from the northwest," the first replied.

"I heard there was quite an earthquake up by Bethel. Probably cut their vacation short," replied the other.

CHAPTER 29

CELEBRATION

Tom and Jerry were just beginning their meal at the hotel when Sam, Bill and Jimmy came in with duffle bags in hand.

"Hey guys... Didn't expect you this evening... Glad you're here, right where we started out... Sit down...," called Tom.

They pulled another table over and all sat down to order.

"Where's Bob?" Tom asked.

"Bob checked himself in at the hospital... Needed a few stitches... Thinks he has a couple of broken bones... Said he would meet us on the ramp at 0900... Guess he's catching a flight down to St Louis around 11:00 A.M. tomorrow," stated Bill.

"I suppose you're heading south as well Bill?" asked Tom.

"Sure am. Gotta get back home... Cindy's been a little nervous not hearing from me for three days," he answered.

"What about your 206?" Jerry asked.

"It's still on floats getting some repairs at Tim's place and should be ready to go in a week or so. I plan to bring Cindy up to pick up the plane and either fly it home or maybe even stay in the Bethel area for a while."

"Good luck no matter which direction you take," said Tom.

As they were eating, the Colonel walked in the door.

"Come join us Colonel Bill," called Tom from their table across the room.

The guys waved him over.

He ordered as well and enjoyed spending some time with his new comrades.

"Colonel... Sam, Bob and Jimmy all broke their airplanes. Are you planning to stick to your word about replacing them?" asked Tom.

"You bet... Already on their way," he replied.

"We actually had to order 10 of those from Cessna to make it worth their while," he stated.

"That's awesome," responded Tom.

"What about Bucks?" he asked.

"Didn't consider that one," the Colonel replied.

"Well... no need to bring up another aircraft, but a generous equitable donation to his grandkids college fund might be a good thing." stated Tom.

"Ok... You've got it," agreed the colonel.

Sam, "What are your plans? asked Tom.

Sam glanced over at the Colonel, "Instead of one of those new 206's, I'd like to have that helicopter parked in the hangar at Tim's.

"That helicopter doesn't exist," stated the Colonel.

Tom broke in, "Well that should make the trade easy." as he glanced at the Colonel.

"You know. I suppose it would... New paint, interior... okay...," agreed the Colonel.

Sam smiled broadly and high fived Tom, "Alright!"

"Tom," continued the Colonel.

"Why don't you take the original blue and white 206 for now... Let us make the repairs on yours... Looked pretty rough on the ramp... Probably take a couple of weeks or so," suggested the Colonel.

"Sounds good Colonel. Thanks," answered Tom.

The Colonel continued as he looked over at Sam, "We have another one you can borrow Sam. I imagine you'd like some transportation for a bit until we can get your helicopter 'refurbished and registered."

"That would be outstanding Colonel. Like to fly Mae home in the morning," answered Sam.

"Bill... Jerry... We can get new colors back on your aircraft at your convenience," mentioned the Colonel.

"What about you Iceman?" asked Jerry.

"Well... Probably like to make a bunch of stops heading south... Take my time gettin' back to Georgia," Tom continued.

"Think I'll set up an Alaska Bush Flying school. Flight instructing down at the Lake sounds pretty good about now," he concluded.

"And you Jerry?" asked Tom.

"I'm just moving the aircraft over to Merrill Field in the morning... Closer to home," he stated.

The dinner turned into a celebration, however, Tom as well as Sam had occasional thoughts of yet another short war survived and the tragedies therein.

Chapter 30

GOODBYE ALASKA?

The next morning, Bob, with a cast on his wrist extending down his hand on one side, Sam, Jimmy, Bill, Jerry and Tom met on the ramp.

After some discussion, Bob, Jimmy and Bill soon left for the terminal to catch flights to St Louis, Reno and Phoenix.

Jerry and Sam had remained for a few minutes to see Tom off.

After their strong handshakes and military style hugs, they separated to walk toward their aircraft.

As Tom ambled over toward his blue and white Cessna, he called back, "Come on down South for a visit anytime... Darn good fishing."

"Will do," answered Sam.

Tom climbed aboard, pulled his door shut and opened the window.

"Thanks again guys. Enjoy that 206 Jerry."

"Can't wait to ride in that helicopter someday Sam... See you boys later," as he closed his window.

They both gave a low 'see you later' type wave.

A moment later, he started the engine and began his taxi to the runway.

Both Sam and Jerry stepped around the front of their aircraft and watched Tom taxi out of sight.

Shortly, they watched his take off from runway 25 R and continued to watch as he crossed the Cook Inlet.

The two watched him bank off to the right and it appeared he'd planned a southeast departure once he had adequate altitude.

Jerry mentioned quietly, "I sure hate to see him go."

"Yeah," said Sam.

As they turned back to their aircraft, Jerry glanced once more to catch a last glimpse of Tom's departing plane.

The bright morning sun had broken over the top of the Chugach Range and was shining brightly and reflecting on the waters of the Cook Inlet.

"Where'd he go Sam?" Jerry called.

With no aircraft in site, they both looked back West.

Suddenly, Jerry spotted the sun reflecting off the wings of Tom's plane, "Where the heck is he going Sam?" - Looks like he's heading northwest toward the Alaska Range!"

"I think you're right Jerry," Sam replied... "My guess is that he's headed back to Farewell to hook up with Jediah to track down some aliens."

"Or, maybe he's headed up toward the Innoco River to dig up that treasure he's always talked about," mentioned Jerry.

"Or... Maybe both...," surmised Sam.

Captain Tom, now out of 5,000 feet, glanced over his left shoulder at Mt Susitna, the 'Sleeping Lady', "Always had a thing for that lady."

He smiled, then kicked on his XM Radio to find one of his favorite singers - Neil Young.

"Long may you run...," Neil wailed.

Again he smiled as he had hit on one of his favorite songs as well.

With autopilot on, he continued toward the brilliant snow covered peaks of the Alaska Range.

The two stood together and continued to watch until Tom was completely out of sight.

They were quiet, thoughtful, then traded glances, shook their heads and smiled.

"Let's go to Farewell," they said in unison.

"Soon..." as they thought of their wives and families.

"Wild Bill's gonna' be mad," suggested Jerry.

"Tom's gonna' be surprised to see us," Sam suggested.

"No he won't," concluded Jerry.

They laughed, shook hands, hugged and slapped each other on the back, turned and headed toward their aircraft with a spring in their step.

Once a Warrior- Always a Warrior

Freedom is not Free!

Thank a Veteran Today!

REMEMBRANCE OF FRIENDS AND COMRADES

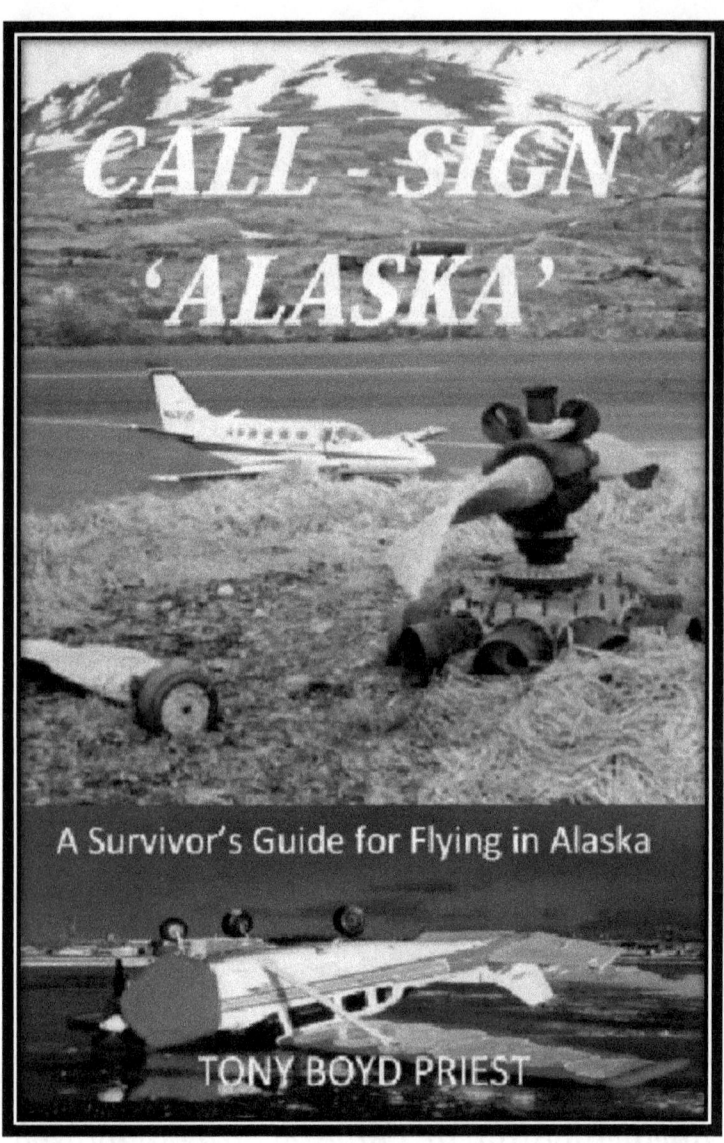

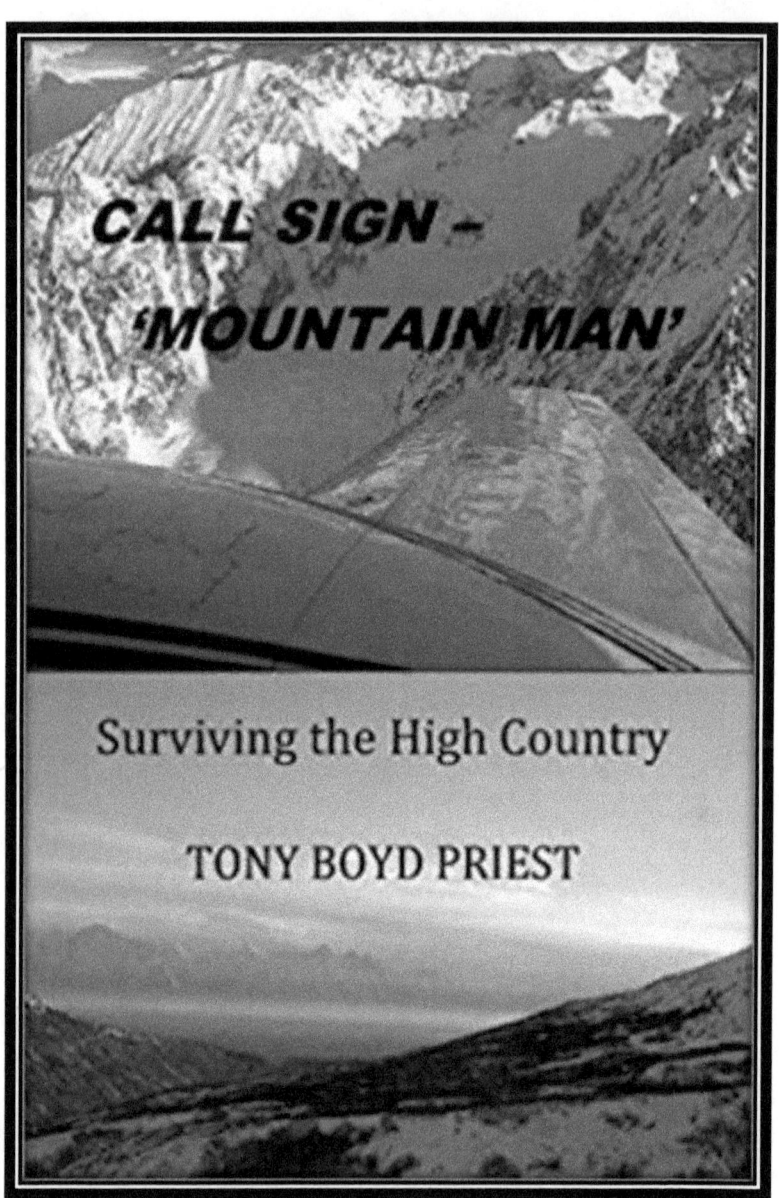

Dear Alaska,

What an awesome privilege it was for me to fly through your beautiful mountain passes, over the vastness of your tundra and to see your pristine rivers, lakes and islands.

I've soaked into my soul the canvas of the soft pastel colors of your skies touting the complete spectrum of the colors of the rainbow.

I've sailed along past your majestic, snowcapped mountains and seen a thousand of your beautiful sunrises and sunsets of yellows, gold's and reds, sometimes at the hour of midnight.

I've sailed over your deep, aqua blue, sometimes emerald green waters strewn with the brilliant whiteness of the ice. Your crystal clear rivers, sometimes placid, were often raging as they weaved through your pristine wilderness.

I've seen firsthand the unstoppable forces of nature, humbling even the strongest and heartiest of souls.

I've watched as millions of sea birds all took flight at the same time, changing the colors of the landscape from green and blue to white.

I've shared with my kindred Alaskan people, sadness and loss, but also happiness and good cheer.

Thank You Alaska for sharing your Great Land, your wonderful people, your mystery and your challenge.

Thank You God, for allowing me to be there and to become an integral part of your beautiful Creation. Amen.

Tony Boyd Priest
June 28, 1990

www.ingramcontent.com/pod-product-compliance
Lightning Source LLC
Chambersburg PA
CBHW061427040426
42450CB00007B/936